ALEX'S RESTAURANT

Cartoons
By Peter Sinclair

The Crossing Press, Freedom, Ca 95019

To my parents, who showed me courage. To my wife who is trying to teach me patience. To my children, who are keeping me honest. To Jay Kennedy, for being ahead of his time. To Britt Eustis, and my sister and Sinclair for egging me on. To Mary Wolf and Bob Thibodeau for helping with the timing, and to Dennis Hayes for steering me along.

Cover cartoon and design by Peter Sinclair
Book design by Amy Sibiga

Printed in the U.S.A.

Library of Congress Cataloging-in Publication Data

Sinclair, Peter (Peter William), 1953-
Alex's restaurant : cartoons / by Peter Sinclair.
p. cm.
ISBN 0-89594-647-5. -- ISBN 0-89594-578-9 (pbk.)
I. Title.
PN6727.S528A43 1993
741.5'973--dc20
93-25853
CIP

Foreword

The future has arrived, and it is not what it used to be.

During my lifetime, our vision of "the future" has swung from the gee whiz futurama, to mellow whole earth ecotopia, to burned out blade runner mondo 2000.

Well, we're into it now, for better or worse. The post-industrial age, the communications age, the information age, the Aquarian age, the greening of America, the harmonic convergence, the archaic revival, the new millenium. Not one or the other, but all at the same time, each one changing so fast that things are bumping into each other in ways that seem odd and oxymoronic.

Computer astrology, ginseng beer, laser acupuncture, samurai salesmen, virtual reality, aerobic yoga, and rune stones, high tech shamans, biofeedback meditation, electric didjereedoo, herbal deodorant, organic petfood, *I Ching* for managers, psychic phone service, fire walking at the Holiday Inn, a drumming circle at the Sheraton.

We are seeing the future, and it is weird. And, I hope, funny, because this is what Alex's is all about.

Peter Sinclair

Introduction

Peter Sinclair is a man after my own art. As a fellow traveler in the humor potential movement, Peter realizes the potential humor has to shed light on Life's Great Question: *Does existence have any intrinsic significance, or are we just the comedy channel for the Gods?*

In a culture where junk-food ideas are the usual fare, Peter has chosen as his arena *Alex's*, a health food restaurant. There, he serves up all of the great philosophical and psychological themes, from holism to chocoholism.

Alex's is a welcome sanctuary for the weary seeker who has tried so many paths he is pathological, had so much personal growth that he's totally growthed out, and has expanded his mind so much that he can no longer fit through his front door.

But *Alex's* also appeals to those who think that "new age" is what you are on your next birthday, and personal growth is something that happens between Thanksgiving and New Year's and can best be measured on a bathroom scale.

Drop in at *Alex's* and you're likely to find owner Alex, who is beginning to suspect that there is indeed a seeker born every minute and two to take him along the path; Alex's kitchen help Cranbrook, who is living proof that the ozone layer hasn't been completely destroyed; and Carl, a blue-collar type with an overflowing skeptic system, who finds whole grain foods and whole grain ideas mostly indigestible.

Now it is true that *Alex's* may be a bit ahead of its time. But there is proof that the world is catching up. For example, a recent survey showed that 40% of the Americans questioned believe that tofu is the food of the future (although 80% of them want to keep it that way). The same study showed that 35% of Americans believe in reincarnation. (Even more amazing, 15% of those who do not believe in reincarnation report that they did in their last lifetime.)

So while we may have to wait a few years before Dagwood follows Robert Bly into the woods and takes a primal drumming workshop, or Cathy gets rolfed and runs away with a Native American shaman, or Mary Worth takes the EST training, or Garfield and John finally recognize their codependence and seek counseling—*Alex's* is here and now.

Sure, the world is in a grave state. But the best way to overcome gravity is with levity. So fix yourself a heaping bowl of crunchy granola, slip on a pair of Tibetan meditation slippers, put on Yanni's latest tape (I think it's called *Yanni Be Good*), and get ready to laugh. Or, put this book in the bathroom, and if you're on one of those high fiber diets that Alex recommends, you can be a regular reader of *Alex's*. It's a fact. Four out of five humorologists recommend *Alex's* as a daily laughsitive, guaranteed to provide regularhilarity and prevent humorrhoids.

May the FARCE be with you,
Steve Bhaerman
aka Swami Beyondananda

AHEM... SO!... YOU WANT TO START UP A... A SO-CALLED HEALTH FOOD RESTAURANT?
YES, SIR.
LOAN DEPT.

ACTUALLY, IT'S MORE THAN THAT.....

I THINK OF IT AS A STARTING POINT FOR PEOPLE TO BEGIN HEALTHIER, HAPPIER, LONGER AND MORE PRODUCTIVE LIVES!

HMMMM.....

SO YOU THINK THERE'S A DEMAND FOR THAT?
I ADMIT IT'S A RISK.....
3-26
PETER SINCLAIR

THIS DOESN'T SEEM LIKE THE LIKELIEST NEIGHBORHOOD TO START A HEALTH FOOD RESTAURANT.
ANGELO'S BAR & GRILL
3-27

YEAH, BUT THIS PLACE IS FOR SALE-- CHEAP.....
HEY, ANGELO!...
... JUST MAKE IT THE USUAL... DOUBLE CHEESE BACO-BURGER, FRIES WITH GRAVY, AND A SHAKE....

HONEY, I FEEL A SENSE OF MISSION.....
HEY, PAL..... YA GOTTA LIGHT?

HELP WANTED

MAY I HELP YOU?

CRANBROOK WILSON REPORTING TO JOIN THE WORKFARCE, YER HONOR.
3-28

MY DESIRE TO WORK IS, OF COURSE, PURELY INTELLECTUAL. I WANT TO STUDY AND EXPERIENCE THE GRIM, DRONE-LIKE EXISTENCE OF THE WAGE SLAVE....

THE QUIET DESPERATION TO WHICH MOST OF MY FELLOW MEN ARE RESIGNED... THE SMOLDERING NEUROSIS AND ANXIETY OF THEIR BANAL EXISTENCES

WELL... WE DO NEED SOME HELP GETTING THINGS OFF THE GROUND.....
GREAT!

CAN I GET MY FIRST CHECK IN ADVANCE?
KITCHEN
3-29

MORNING, ANGELO... JUST MAKE IT THE USUAL...
3-30

UURRFF!

WHAT'S HAPPENING? WHERE'S ANGELO?
HE'S GONE. MY NAME'S ALEX AND I JUST BOUGHT THIS PLACE

SO YOU'RE OPENING A GREENHOUSE?
A RESTAURANT. AND WE'RE CHANGING THE AMBIENCE. YOU THINK THE PLANTS ARE TOO MUCH?

... SINCE WE'LL BE SERVING MOSTLY VEGETARIAN FOOD.....

... WE THOUGHT THE PLANTS WOULD BE THE FIRST THING TO BRING IN....
VEGETARIAN?

... TO HELP OUR CLIENTELE FEEL MORE AT HOME,
OH,,... YEAH.

GREAT. HE'S OPENING A RESTAURANT FOR TREE SLOTHS.
3-31

SO CARL, WHAT WAS THIS PLACE LIKE BEFORE ALEX BOUGHT IT?

OH! GREATEST LITTLE GREASY SPOON YOU EVER SAW! IT WAS CALLED ANGELO'S!

ANGELO WAS A TWO FISTED, NO NONSENSE BURGER FLIPPER WITH KETCHUP IN HIS VEINS!

... AND THEY HAD THIS GREAT WAITRESS,... WANDA,..... REAL CLASSY, YOU KNOW, WITH THE BIG HAIR!

MORE COFFEE?

I GUESS THE GOOD THINGS NEVER CHANGE.

EVERY GREAT CHEF MUST MASTER THE CRAFT OF BREAD MAKING....

A GOOD HONEST BREAD IS NOT ONLY THE STAFF OF LIFE....
SINCLAIR

... IN FACT, A FINE LOAF OF BREAD IS ALSO A WORK OF ART!
BLOP

WELL, ALEX, YOURS CERTAINLY SUCCEEDS AS SCULPTURE....
...REMINDS ME OF A CERAMIC PIECE I DID ONCE....
TAP TAP

I THINK THE KEY TO MOVING THIS BREAD WILL BE A STRONG PRODUCT IMAGE!
YOU MEAN, LIKE THE MARLBORO MAN?

SORT OF. I'M CALLING IT "SOURDOUGH LUMBERJACK BREAD." HOW MUCH DO WE HAVE NOW?

ABOUT A CORD AND A HALF
SO... WE RUN A SALE ON TOAST
SINCLAIR
4-3

SOMETIMES I WORRY THIS BUSINESS WILL MAKE ME A "TYPE A"

NO PROBLEM HERE! I'M "TYPE B", ALL THE WAY!
4-4

SINCLAIR

IS THERE A "TYPE X"?

THIS IS "THE WAY OF THE WARRIOR-JANITOR."
SLOP ....MOP..

BY BEING TOTALLY AWARE, I BECOME ONE WITH MY WORK.....

MOP MOP
SINCLAIR

I BECOME ONE WITH THE MOP,.... I BECOME ONE WITH THE........
MOP! SLOP!
4-5

WANT TO TRY SOME AMARANTH.... THE MAYAN SUPERGRAIN?

HOW 'BOUT SOME QUINOA..... SACRED FOOD OF THE INCAS?

ACTUALLY, I'D LIKE SOME KIELBASA.......

MYSTERIOUS MEAL OF THE POLISH.
SINCLAIR
4-6

INTERESTING. SOME SCIENTISTS SAY THE HOLE IN THE OZONE LAYER MIGHT BE CLOSING!

GEE,...YOU'D BETTER GET BACK THROUGH, OR YOU'LL NEVER MAKE IT HOME.
SINCLAIR
4-7

OUR SPECIAL ALL THIS WEEK IS A MEAL BASED ON THE STAPLES OF THE ABORIGINAL BUSHMEN!

IT INCLUDES, MANIOC PIE, CATTAIL ROOTS, WILD LEEK BROTH, CRUNCHY ROSE HIP PILAF,...

JERUSALEM ARTICHOKES, ..PRICKLY PEAR JUICE,...

.... STEAMED PURSLANE, BURDOCK ROOT, AND TINY COCKTAIL SHRIMP SALAD!

THE ABORIGINAL BUSHMEN ATE TINY COCKTAIL SHRIMP?

WELL, NO, BUT WE COULD'NT GET ANY WITCHETY GRUBS.

GRAND OPENING
OUR FIRST DAY IN BUSINESS!
SINCLAIR

I'VE DREAMED OF OWNING A HEALTH CLUB FOR YEARS! I WANT TO CELEBRATE SOMEHOW!
HOW'S THIS? I GUARANTEE TO MAKE A NEW PERSON OUT OF THE NEXT GUY WHO COMES IN THAT DOOR!
KNOCK KNOCK

HI! DID YOU FOLKS ORDER THE VEGGIE PLATTER WITH TOFU-TOTS?
4-9

FRIEND, THIS IS YOUR LUCKY DAY! HOW WOULD YOU LIKE TO CHANGE YOUR LIFE?
SINCLAIR
MEGA-FITNESS PLUS CAN HELP YOU ACTUALIZE YOUR DREAMS!!

THINK OF IT! EVERYONE HAS A HIDDEN DREAM... A THEME IN THEIR LIFE... SUBLIME PURPOSE!! WHAT'S YOURS?

DESTROY ALL MONSTERS?
GOOD! THAT'S.... REAL GOOD!.....AND MEGA-FITNESS CAN HELP!!
4-10

WE'RE TURNING YOU OVER TO OUR "MASS BUILDING EXPERT, "ROIDZ"...

"ROIDZS"... NOW LET'S SEE... THAT WOULD BE SHORT FOR... ANDROID?

...POLAROID? HUMANOID? METEOROID?

STEROID?
HI BOSS!.... HEY! WHO'S THE PENCILNECK?

YOUR FIRST PROJECT.

WELL, I MIGHT AS WELL SHOW YOU AROUND AND HAVE YOU MEET THE STAFF.
WORKOUT ROOM
MEGAFIT

HEY GROUP! THIS IS CRANBROOK. HE'S MY FIRST CLIENT!!

HI! I'M CHIP!
HI! I'M FLIP!
HI! I'M BOBBY!
MEGA FIT

I'M CUBBY!
I'M ANNETTE!
SO, I'VE ENTERED THE LAIR OF THE SURF NAZIS!
GREAT BUNCH, EH?

SO... YOU WORK AT THE HEALTH FOOD PLACE?
YUP. ALEX'S.
MEGA-FIT

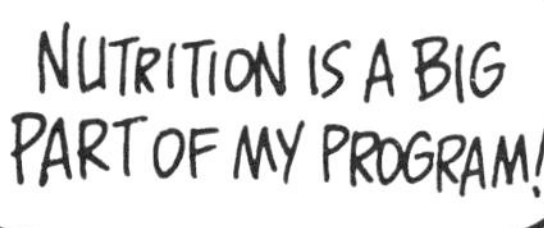
NUTRITION IS A BIG PART OF MY PROGRAM!

MEGAFIT

I FOLLOW THE DIET IN THIS BOOK
MEGA-FIT

"EAT TO KICK BUTT"?
YOU CAN BORROW IT IF YOU WANT

YOU KNOW, MY BRAIN WORKS IN FUNNY WAYS. I GUESS IT'S "MATH ANXIETY." I MEAN, JUST MENTION A NUMBER, AND..... I LIKE, GO BLANK!

HMMM....

FOUR.

YOU KNOW, MY BRAIN WORKS IN FUNNY WAYS. I GUESS IT'S "MATH ANXIETY." I MEAN, JUST MENTION A NUMBER, AND..... I LIKE, GO BLANK!

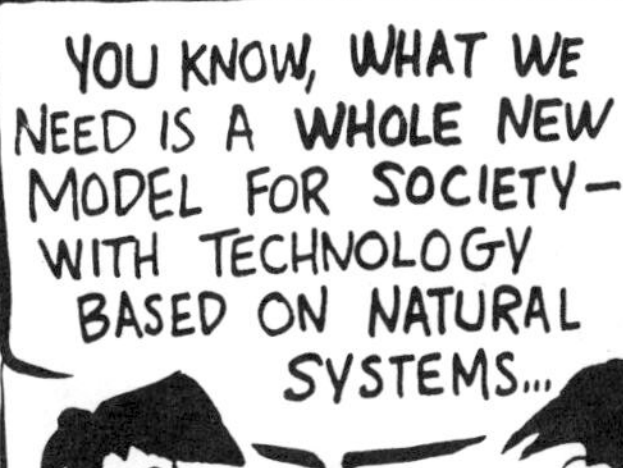
YOU KNOW, WHAT WE NEED IS A WHOLE NEW MODEL FOR SOCIETY— WITH TECHNOLOGY BASED ON NATURAL SYSTEMS...

... AND IN HARMONY WITH OTHER FORMS OF LIFE!
SINCLAIR

IT'S BEEN DONE.

HAVE YOU EVER SEEN THE FLINTSTONES?
4-30

WOULD YOU LIKE DRESSING WITH YOUR SALAD?
SINCLAIR

WE HAVE FRENCH, ITALIAN, THOUSAND ISLAND AND EXXON.

5-1

WHAT'S "EXXON" DRESSING?

OH, WE JUST DUMP OIL ALL OVER YOU.

OH YEAH? WELL, YOU'RE JUST NUTS, THAT'S ALL, JUST PLAIN CRAZY!!
SINCLAIR
5-2

KNOW WHAT YOU NEED? A REALITY CHECK! HAVE YOU CONSIDERED A REALITY CHECK?

IT'S IN THE MAIL.

I GOT THAT PART-TIME JOB WITH THE SCHOOL SYSTEM!

GREAT, JOANNE, SO YOU'LL NEED TUESDAYS OFF...
YEAH, I'LL BE GOING INTO ALL THE THIRD GRADE CLASSES....
SINCLAIR

GREAT!
ISN'T IT? I'LL FINALLY BE ABLE TO USE MY DEGREE!
5-3

O.K., CLASS, PUT YOUR BOOKS AWAY.... IT'S TIME FOR A SPECIAL VISITOR ... THE STRESS REDUCTION LADY!

DID YOU HEAR ABOUT CRANBROOK'S NEWEST PROJECT?

HE SIGNED UP WITH "PEN PALS FOR PEACE" TO GET A RUSSIAN PEN PAL!
WOW! THAT'S GREAT!

IT'S A GREAT WAY FOR THOSE PEOPLE TO GET A CLEARER PICTURE OF AMERICAN LIFE!
SINCLAIR

"....WELL, THAT'S ABOUT IT FOR NOW, YURI, I'M OFF TO PRACTICE AGAIN. AS YOU KNOW, I PLAY QUARTERBACK IN MY ROCK-AND-ROLL BAND...."
5-4

HEY, ROIDZ, YOU GOT ANY OF THOSE PICTURES OF YOU POSING AT THE MR. AKRON CONTEST?
TRAINER
SINCLAIR

WELL, I JUST HAPPEN TO HAVE A FEW LEFT.
GREAT! CAN I HAVE ONE?

GEE, THE LITTLE GUY REALLY LOOKS UP TO ME!
TRAINER

"DEAR YURI,
HERE'S THAT PICTURE OF ME YOU ASKED FOR. OF COURSE, I'M NOT ALWAYS THIS TAN! HA! HA!"
5-5

NO MATTER WHAT YOU SAY, I'M STILL A REAGAN DEMOCRAT!

HMMM..... I'M SORT OF A FRANK ZAPPA LIBERTARIAN.

MARXIST-LENTILIST.
SINCLAIR 4-23

DID YOU EVER WISH YOU KNEW THEN WHAT YOU KNOW NOW?

TRUTHFULLY, I'M NOT SURE I FULLY NOW KNOW WHAT I KNOW EVEN NOW. SO HOW COULD I KNOW IF IT WOULD HAVE HELPED ME TO KNOW IT THEN?

SINCLAIR
4-24

I GUESS YOU'RE RIGHT.
I KNOW.

AMAZING! "3 OUT OF 4 AMERICANS ARE UNABLE TO GRASP SIMPLE MATHEMATICAL CONCEPTS"!
DAILY NEWS

?

IS THAT A LOT?
SINCLAIR 4-25

HI! I'M FROM THE DAILY NEWS! WE'RE GOING TO DO A STORY ABOUT YOUR RESTAURANT!

WE'RE CALLING IT, "NATURAL FOOD: IT'S NOT JUST FOR CRANKS, BURNOUTS AND WEIRDOS ANYMORE!"

CAN YOU EXCUSE ME A MOMENT?

EMPLOYEES ONLY

HEY, CRANBROOK! HOW WOULD YOU LIKE A DAY OFF?
GREAT!

ROIDZ, I THINK HE SAID OAT BRAN, NOT OAT BRAIN....

CRANBROOK, SOMETIMES I HAVE TROUBLE REMEMBERING WHAT YOUR JOB IS AROUND HERE ANYHOW.

WELL, THAT'S INTERESTING! YOU KNOW, THE HOPI INDIANS HAD NO WORD FOR "JOB"
I BET THEY DIDN'T HAVE A WORD FOR "UNEMPLOYMENT" EITHER!

I WONDER IF THE HOPIS HAD A WORD FOR "GROVELLING"?

HEY, WAITER! THERE'S A BUG IN MY SALAD!

YES, OUR RESTAURANT PLAYS HOST TO A RICH DIVERSITY OF LIFE IN AN INTRICATE WEB OF ECOLOGICAL WHOLENESS.

5-14

YOU MAY BE ASSURED THIS LITTLE FELLOW'S EXISTENCE IS **PROOF** OF THE PURE ORGANIC ENVIRONMENT WE MAINTAIN IN OUR KITCHEN.

SINCLAIR
HEY, PAL, I'VE LEARNED IT'S BEST JUST TO **EAT** THE DARN THINGS.

MAY I RECOMMEND THE "SOURDOUGH LUMBERJACK BREAD," MA'AM?

DOES IT HAVE LOTS OF **FIBER?**

FIBER? MA'AM, THIS BREAD WILL EXPAND YOUR INTESTINAL CONSCIOUSNESS!
SINCLAIR

PUT IT THIS WAY. IF THERE'S ANY LEFTOVER ON SATURDAY, ALEX IS USING IT TO BUILD A **DECK.**
5-15

I SEE YOU GOT SOME OF THOSE "PUMP" SNEAKERS!...
SINCLAIR

5-16
I THINK YOU'VE GOT 'EM A LITTLE **OVERINFLATED.....**
WEIGHT ROOM

HOW ARE YOUR "PUMP" SNEAKERS WORKING OUT?
SINCLAIR

I HAD A BLOWOUT!
5-17

THIS IS TODAY'S SPECIAL, CARL. IT SHOULD HAVE A RELAXING EFFECT ON YOU.

IT LOOKS LIKE POND SCUM.
WELL, TO THE UNINITIATED, PERHAPS.

MORE PROPERLY... IT'S GOURMET-STYLE, BLUE-GREEN ALGAE.
YOU MEAN... I'M RIGHT? IT'S POND SCUM?!

YOU WANT ME TO EAT POND SCUM? YOU'RE SERVING POND SCUM? HEY! EVERYBODY! LOOKY HERE! CHECK IT OUT! POND SCUM!!!
5-18

HERE YOU GO.

A NEW IDEA I HAD WAS TO LET THE CUSTOMERS CLEAN UP AND WASH THEIR OWN DISHES.

I FEEL THAT THIS WILL PROVIDE YOU WITH A VERY GROUNDING, CENTERING AND NURTURING EXPERIENCE.

MAY I SPEAK TO YOU FOR A MOMENT?
COULDN'T WE JUST HOLD HANDS IN A CIRCLE OR SOMETHING?
5-19

I ORDERED SOME OF THE "HOMEMADE" BREAD AND SOME SOUP.

JUST A MINUTE, I'LL SLICE THAT BREAD FOR YOU.

I WONDER WHY THEY CALL IT "LUMBERJACK BREAD"?

RRRRRRR
RRRUNNNRUNNR
SINCLAIR
5-21

HEY, ALEX, THAT "NEW AGE" PRODUCTS SALESMAN IS HERE

SIGH

WELL, WHAT DO YOU HAVE FOR ME TODAY?
ONLY THE LATEST IN WHOLISTIC MIND-BODY PRODUCTS!

I HOPE THIS IS BETTER THAN THE QUARTZ CRYSTAL SUPPOSITORIES.
HEY, WE'VE SOLD A LOT OF THOSE..

HERE'S OUR NEWEST MIND-BODY PRODUCT...THE NEUROLODEON! AN ELECTRONIC MIND-EXPANSION DEVICE!
5-24

LIGHT PULSES AND SOUNDS TO ENTRAIN THE BRAIN WAVES IN ALTERED STATES!
SINCLAIR

IT'S MEDITATION MADE EASY!

THINK OF IT AS SCRUBBING BUBBLES FOR YOUR NEURONS!

THESE BRAIN-MIND MACHINES MAY ACTUALLY **INCREASE** INTELLIGENCE!

WOW! HOW MUCH ARE THEY?
10,000 DOLLARS.

ONLY AN **IDIOT** WOULD PAY THAT MUCH FOR ONE OF THOSE!

EXACTLY! THAT'S HOW WE TARGET THE NEEDIEST INDIVIDUALS!
5·23

YOU KNOW, THERE'S AN OLD YUGOSLAVIAN PROVERB....

"A GOOD **REST** IS HALF THE WORK."

NO WONDER YOUR WORK IS ALWAYS **HALF DONE.**
5·25

HEY, WAITER! THERE'S A **BUG** IN MY SALAD!

5·26

CRUNCH CRUNCH CRUNCH

CARL'S STILL HAVING TROUBLE ADJUSTING TO THE REDUCED PROTEIN INTAKE.
COULDN'T WE JUST GET HIM SOME 'BACO-BITS'?

HEY,... WAITER! THERE'S A BUG IN MY SALAD!
5·28

NO PROBLEM! WITH THIS PRAYING MANTIS, OUR NEW NATURAL PEST CONTROL,... BUGS ARE A THING OF THE PAST!

SIC 'EM, SHEEBA!
ZIP!

WHEN SHE'S DONE, IT'S A GOOD IDEA TO TIP HER WITH A CROUTON OR SOMETHING......

I COULDN'T HELP HEARING THAT YOUR BUSINESS IS A LITTLE SLOW! MY CARD.

CHAD UPLINK... ADVERTISING... PUBLIC RELATIONS
YUP. MY FIRM IS SETTING UP A BRANCH HERE.

I'VE SEEN YOU BEFORE...
HMMM, MAYBE AT THE LAST "WORKAHOLICS ANONYMOUS" MEETING,...
5·29

YOU WERE THE GUY WITH THE LAPTOP!
EXACTLY!

LOOK, IF YOU WANT TO BRING IN MORE CUSTOMERS, YOU'VE GOT TO BROADEN YOUR APPEAL TO THE AVERAGE GUY!

I'VE TRIED THAT...
TARGET YOUR AUDIENCE! HERE'S WHERE MARKETING STRATEGY COMES IN!

YOUR AVERAGE MAN ON THE STREET SHOULD BE ABLE TO SAY... MY TRUCK, MY GIRL... MY BEER,..., AND MY.... UH... CHICK-PEAS OR SOMETHIN'.
MAKES SENSE!
OR, LIKE, "COME TO BEAN CURD COUNTRY"!
EXACTLY! LET'S JOT SOME OF THESE DOWN!
5·30

A TV CAMPAIGN WOULD HELP YOU MAKE PEOPLE COMFORTABLE WITH FOOD THEY'RE NOT USED TO.

BUT HOW?
A PRODUCT'S A PRODUCT! YOU SELL IT JUST LIKE SOAP, CIGARETTES OR BEER!

YOU NEED PEOPLE TO LOOK AT YOUR CUISINE IN A NEW AND INTERESTING WAY.... SOMETHING THEY HAVEN'T THOUGHT OF BEFORE!

HOW 'BOUT, "SEAWEED..... IT'S NOT JUST FOR BREAKFAST ANYMORE"?
NOW YOU'RE COOKIN'!

THAT GUY REALLY WANTS TO SELL ME ON ADVERTISING...

BUT I WONDER WHY WE JUST SHOULDN'T RELY ON WORD OF MOUTH....

WELL, THE WORD IS YOU'RE A BUNCH OF WEIRDOS AND YOU'RE GONNA FOLD!
WELL, I SUPPOSE WE COULD USE SOME IMAGE-BUILDING....
YOU GOT THAT RIGHT.

HOLY TOMOLEY!
!!!!!!

RELAX! THAT'S OUR NEW PRAYING MANTIS! "THE NATURAL WAY TO KEEP ROACHES AT BAY!"
?

WELL, I THINK IT MUSTA FINISHED OFF THE ROACHES.
WHY?

'CUZ,.. NOW IT'S STARTING ON MY PITA SANDWICH.
MUNCH!

ENDLESS HOURS SPENT AT A COMPUTER SCREEN..... SO MANY OF US SPEND OUR LIVES AT WORK AND PLAY.....

..... LOST IN THE FLICKER OF ELECTRONS ON A PHOSPHOR AND PLASTIC SCREEN. IT'S POIGNANT AND TERRIFYING!
SINCLAIR

BUT, YOU KNOW WHAT THEY SAY.....

LIFE IS TERMINAL.
DON'T YOU HAVE SOME OTHER WORK YOU COULD BE DOING?
6-4

I'VE BEEN STUDYING THE MATING HABITS OF PRAYING MANTISES.

ONCE SHE FINDS THAT "SPECIAL GUY", SHE MUST QUICKLY DESTROY HIS BRAIN BEFORE SHE MATES WITH HIM.
6-5

OF COURSE, HUMAN FEMALES ARE DIFFERENT, RIGHT, DEAR?
SINCLAIR

YES. EVOLUTION HAS REMOVED THE NECESSITY OF THAT STEP.

LIKE IT? IT'S A PICTURE OF A '59 ELDORADO!
WOW! LOOK AT THE CHROME! AND THE TAIL FINS! THOSE WERE REAL CARS!

MY DAD HAD ONE OF THOSE. I HAVEN'T SEEN ONE IN YEARS!

I'M SENDING IT TO MY RUSSIAN PEN PAL. HE WANTS TO KNOW MORE ABOUT AMERICAN CULTURE.
SINCLAIR

"AND HERE'S A PICTURE OF MY NEW CAR. ALL WORKERS GET A NEW ONE EACH YEAR SO WE CAN CRUISE FOR CHICKS AND BURGERS!"
6-6

I SUPPOSE YOU ALL KNOW WE'VE HAD TROUBLE GAINING ACCEPTANCE AMONG THE REGULARS.

MAYBE WE NEED TO CHANGE OUR APPROACH PSYCHOLOGICALLY.

I'VE BEEN READING A BOOK WHICH MAY HAVE SOME BEARING ON OUR PROBLEM.
IT'S CALLED "ON DEATH AND DIETING" BY ELIZABETH GOBBLER-ROSS.
I'VE HEARD OF THAT BOOK!
SINCLAIR
6-7
THIS BOOK SAYS TO CHANGE THEIR LIFESTYLES WE NEED TO DEAL WITH THE "INNER CHILD" IN ALL OUR CUSTOMERS.
ON DEATH AND DIETING
SINCLAIR
"INSIDE EVERY MAN IS A SMALL BOY TRYING TO BECOME INDEPENDENT.
CARL! EAT YOUR GREENS!

BUT I HATE BROCCOLI.

" IN TODAY'S WORLD, EVEN ADULTS HAVE LITTLE CHANCE FOR SELF-EXPRESSION...
KRYZYZNIAK! GET TO WORK OR GET OUT!

"LEAVING FOOD AS ONE OF THE ONLY AREAS OF CONTROL."
GET THIS BROCCOLI OFF MY PLATE!
6-8

SO... HOW DOES ELIZABETH GOBBLER-ROSS DEAL WITH CHANGING PEOPLE'S EATING HABITS?

WELL, AT HER SEMINARS, SHE INDUCES "OUT-OF-BODY EXPERIENCES" IN HER STUDENTS.....
SINCLAIR
THEY ALL HAVE A CHANCE TO SEE THEMSELVES FROM THE OUTSIDE.....
6-9

NATURALLY.... THEY'RE DISGUSTED.
INCREDIBLE! WHAT A MOTIVATION!

SO ANYHOW, ALEX,.... WHAT ARE YOU GONNA BE WHEN YOU GROW UP?

I OFTEN WONDER THE SAME THING. YOU KNOW, I KEEP GETTING OLDER, BUT I NEVER REALLY FEEL TOTALLY LIKE AN ADULT.

SEEMS LIKE YOU JUST GET MORE UH,... UMM,...

ADULTERATED.
THAT'S IT!
SINCLAIR
6·11

SO, ALEX WAS TELLIN' ME HOW HE LEFT THAT FANCY CORPORATE JOB TO OPEN UP THIS CAFE. WHAT DO YOU THINK MADE HIM DO IT?

WELL, I THINK HE DECIDED IF HE WAS GOING TO BE A BEAN COUNTER....
6·12
SINCLAIR

....HE MIGHT AS WELL BE COUNTING REAL BEANS!
ORGANIC BEANS

IT'S TRUE! BEFORE I BOUGHT THIS CAFE, I WORKED IN A BIG-TIME CORPORATION. I WAS A RISING, AMBITIOUS EXECUTIVE. BUT SOME LITTLE THINGS STARTED TO HAPPEN.....
LIKE WHAT?

..LIKE, I WAS IN THIS "NEW PRODUCTS" MEETING, YOU KNOW, AND I JUST HAPPENED TO SAY, "HEY,....
6·13
SINCLAIR

"..DOES THE WORLD REALLY NEED A NEW DISPOSABLE DIAPER?"
OOH, FAUX PAS BIG TIME!....

SO, ALEX. YOU GAVE UP A CUSHY JOB WITH A BIG CORPORATION, LOTS OF PERKS, AND YOU SINK YOUR SAVINGS INTO THIS DINGY CAFE...

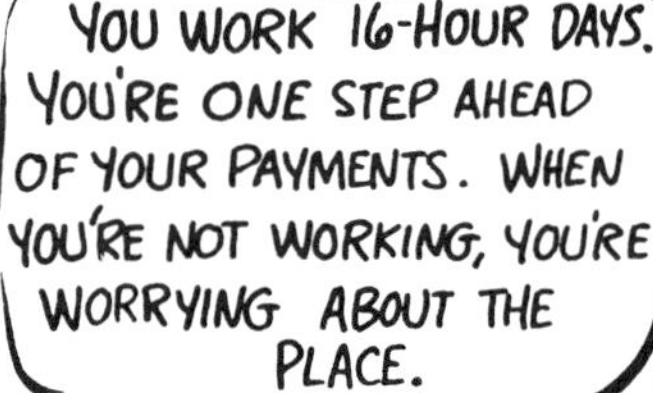

DON'T FORGET TO SHAVE, ALEX. YOU'RE GETTING A LITTLE GRUNGY.
?
SINCLAIR

UGH!
6-18

I WONDER IF ANYONE HATES SHAVING AS MUCH AS I DO?

SIGH......

YOU'RE LATE AGAIN! HOW COME YOU KEEP OVERSLEEPING?

WELL, SEE, I'VE GOT THIS "INNER ALARM CLOCK" THAT ALWAYS WAKES ME UP ON TIME.

SO WHAT'S THE PROBLEM?

I KEEP HITTING MY "INNER SNOOZE BUTTON."
6-19
SINCLAIR

I'M GLAD YOU LIKE OUR STAIR-CLIMBING MACHINE. LOOKS LIKE YOU WERE REALLY GETTING INTO IT.

NEXT TIME, I'LL WARN YOU BEFORE I TURN IT OFF.
SINCLAIR 6-20

O.K! WE FINISHED "BRIDGES" AND "SHRUGS"...

THEN WE DID "CRUNCHES," "SQUATS" AND "DIPS."...

HEY, WHERE'S CRANBROOK?

HE'S IN THE BACK, DOING "HEAVES."
6·21

RICE? BEANS? LENTILS?

NOBODY EATS THIS STUFF ANYMORE!

WHAT DO YOU WANT TO DO? GO BACK 100 YEARS?

I WOULD THINK MORE LIKE 10,000.
YUP. THAT'D BE MORE LIKE IT.
6·22

THIS IS OUR NEW AERO-CYCLE EXER-BIKE.
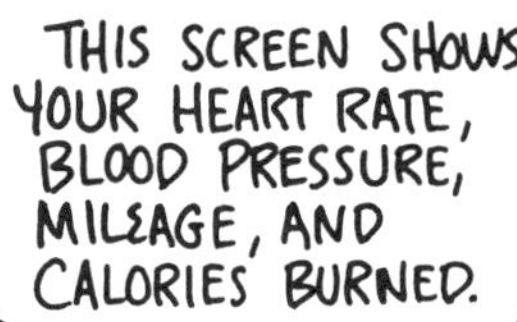
THIS SCREEN SHOWS YOUR HEART RATE, BLOOD PRESSURE, MILEAGE, AND CALORIES BURNED.

BEST OF ALL, IF YOU GET TIRED OF THAT, JUST PRESS THIS BUTTON.
6·23

ROADRUNNER CARTOONS! COOL!

I'VE GIVEN CRANBROOK INCREASED RESPONSIBILITY IN THE KITCHEN.

HE'S GOT SOME INTERESTING NEW IDEAS.
SINCLAIR

RIGHT NOW HE'S WORKING ON A QUICK COOKING METHOD FOR OUR "LUMBERJACK" BREAD
4-16

FIRE IN THE HOLE!!

TODAY WE'RE GOING TO WORK ON SOME NEW MOVEMENTS.

FOR INSTANCE, HAVE I SHOWN YOU DUMBBELL SHRUGS?

4-17

VERY GOOD! HEH HEH HEH!
SINCLAIR

HEH HEE!
A LITTLE GYM RAT HUMOR, I TAKE IT?

QUESTION AUTHORITY
SINCLAIR

QUESTION AUTHORITY
SAYS WHO?
4-18

WELL, I REMEMBERED YOU SAID TO THROW IT AT THE WALL...
SINCLAIR

AND IF IT STICKS, THEN IT'S DONE.

WELL,.. THAT IS THE RULE OF THUMB FOR PASTA.

IT DOESN'T WORK AS WELL FOR PIZZA.
4-19

WELL, CRANBROOK, YOU'VE DONE IT AGAIN. FOULED UP ANOTHER ORDER!

WELL, LIFE IS LIKE A SCHOOL! I TRY TO STUDY MY MISTAKES AND LEARN FROM THEM.

SINCLAIR

THAT'S FINE.

IT JUST SEEMS LIKE YOU'VE BEEN REALLY CRAMMING LATELY.
4-20

O.K., TODAY I'VE GOT A SPECIAL ABDOMINAL SET FOR YOU!
SINCLAIR
4-21

500 STOMACH CRUNCHES!
HOLY COW! THAT'S A LOT!

THINK OF IT AS A TEST OF CHARACTER!

COULDN'T I JUST TAKE A QUIZ?

...RRINGG.....
HELLO?

"LAFFTRON INTERNATIONAL"? I'M SORRY, YOU HAVE THE WRONG...
WAIT!

?
IT'S FOR ME.
6·25
SINCLAIR

LAFFTRON INTERNATIONAL, WHERE OUR BUSINESS IS A JOKE! MAY I HELP YOU?

O.K.,.. WHAT'S LAFFTRON INTERNATIONAL?
MY NEW BUSINESS!

I PROVIDE STRESS REDUCING HUMOR SERVICES TO BIG COMPANIES!

6·26
SINCLAIR

MANY PEOPLE NOW FEEL THAT HUMOR HAS HEALTH BENEFITS!

YOU'RE A CORPORATE JESTER?
I CALL IT STRESS CLOWNSELING!

WELL, CRANBROOK HAS HIS FIRST BIG "CORPORATE JESTER" JOB TODAY. I HOPE HE'S DE-STRESSING ALL THOSE EXECUTIVES!
OH, I'M SURE THEY'RE "DIS-STRESSED" ALL RIGHT!

I'M TELLIN' YA! THESE DAYS EVERYONE'S A WISE GUY! THE OTHER DAY, IN THIS CAFE WHERE I WORK.....
A GUY SAYS TO ME, "HEY, WAITER,... GET ME A RUBBER BAND SANDWICH,.. AND MAKE IT SNAPPY!"
HAH! I'M TELLIN' YA.......
BEEP BEEP
SINCLAIR 6·27

CRANBROOK'S FIRST JOB AS A "CORPORATE JESTER",,,,
HEY! I HOPE THIS ISN'T ONE OF THOSE "DUMMY CORPORATIONS" YOU READ ABOUT?

SERIOUSLY, WHAT ABOUT THAT TRADE DEFICIT? I HEARD OUR LEADING EXPORT IS GARBAGE! HOW'S THAT FOR A GROSS NATIONAL PRODUCT?
OH, I'M TELLIN YA!
HONK

WHICH BRINGS ME TO JAPAN! HEY, HOW 'BOUT THOSE FOOD PRICES OVER THERE? WOW!

THE YEN'S SO HIGH,,,, HEY, THEY DON'T HAVE CAR PAYMENTS, THEY GOT CANTALOUPE PAYMENTS! HA! I'M TELLIN' YA,,,,,
HONK HONK
6·28

SO REMEMBER, HUMOR IS AN IMPORTANT NUTRIENT. AS YOUR CORPORATE JESTER, I FEEL DAILY LAUGHTER IS A VITAL FORM OF EXERCISE.

I CALL MY LAUGH WORKOUTS HUMOR-OBICS!
EXCUSE ME,,,,,

THERE'S JUST ONE THING. YOUR JOKES AREN'T FUNNY.
6·29

WELL, THIS IS "LOW-IMPACT" HUMOR-OBICS.

SO I'VE GOT THIS NEW JOB HELPING CORPORATE TYPES RELAX WITH ON-THE-JOB JOKES!

LAUGHTER IS THE BEST CURE FOR STRESS! AS A CORPORATE JESTER, I'M AN IMPORTANT HEALTH RESOURCE!

I CALL IT STRESS CLOWNSELING! WHATAYA THINK?

I THINK IT'S CLOWNS LIKE YOU THAT GIVE BOZOS A BAD NAME!
6·30

HEY, YOUR ALL DUDED UP! DID YOU JUST COME FROM A **CLOWNING** JOB?
YUP.

GREAT! SO HOW'S BUSINESS?
WELL, THERE'S A **PROBLEM**...

YOU KNOW, I REALLY THOUGHT THIS WAS A GOOD TIME TO BRING THE **HEALING POWER** OF **LAUGHTER** TO THE WORKPLACE.

SO I DEVELOPED MY CONCEPTS OF **CLOWNSELING** AND **HUMOROBICS**! SCIENTISTS SAY THAT HUMOR RELIEVES **STRESS** AND PROMOTES **CREATIVITY**!
SINCLAIR

WELL, THEY ALL **LAUGHED** WHEN I SAID I WAS GOING TO BE A **CLOWN**!

I BET NOBODY'S LAUGHING NOW.
THAT'S THE PROBLEM.

HEY, GUESS WHAT? ME AND THE BOYS ARE GOIN' OUT TONIGHT FOR SOME REAL, BIG-TIME, GREASEBOMB JUNK FOOD AT RIALTO'S.

ARENT YOU WORRIED ABOUT CHOLESTEROL?
NO PROBLEM!

WE'RE TAKING A DESIGNATED JOGGER!
7-2

I'M GOING TO START RENTING THAT SPACE UPSTAIRS FOR MEETINGS AND WORKSHOPS.

WE'VE GOT KIND OF AN INTERESTING GROUP COMING IN TONIGHT! LOOK!

THE "REPUBLICAN ASTROLOGERS"?
THEY SEEM LIKE A NICE BUNCH...
7-3

I CAN'T THANK YOU ENOUGH FOR THE USE OF YOUR SPACE FOR OUR MEETINGS!
NO PROBLEM! SAY, HOW DID YOU HAPPEN TO FORM THE "REPUBLICAN ASTROLOGERS"?

WELL, THE NANCY REAGAN THING HELPED A LOT!
7-4

MANY OF US CAME FROM OTHER FIELDS. I MYSELF WAS AN ECONOMIST... BUT I WAS LOOKING FOR SOMETHING A LITTLE MORE... UH,.. MORE...

..."CONCRETE"?
YES! THAT'S IT!

ALEX'S HOSTS THE FIRST WEEKLY MEETING OF THE "REPUBLICAN ASTROLOGERS",.....
SO, WHAT COULD "ASTRO-ECONOMETRICS" DO FOR ME?

WELL, WE HELP COMPANIES AND INVESTORS ALIGN THEMSELVES WITH THE PLANETS! IN YOUR CASE, FOR INSTANCE,....

WE MIGHT DISCOVER THAT BECAUSE YOUR MARKETING IS IN NEPTUNE,....
7-5

....YOUR PROFITS ARE IN THE TOILET.
BROADLY SPEAKING, YES.
SINCLAIR

GUESS WHAT I STUDIED IN COLLEGE? SOCIOLOGY! WHAT A JOKE, EH?

OH YEAH? MY DEGREE'S IN ANTHROPOLOGY!
HA HA!

?

BACHELOR OF LEISURE STUDIES.
7-6
SINCLAIR

LOOK OUT!
CRASH
TINKLE
OOPS!

THAT'S IT CRANBROOK! YOU'RE FIRED!!
7-7

OF COURSE, THAT MAY SEEM TO BE A SIMPLE SOLUTION TO WHAT IS REALLY A COMPLEX PROBLEM.
SINCLAIR

THESE DAYS PEOPLE ARE LISTENING TO SUBLIMINAL SELF-IMPROVEMENT MESSAGES WITH THEIR MUSIC.

SO THIS NEW RADIO STATION CARRIES THEM IN ALL ITS MUSIC. LIKE, "STOPPING SMOKING IS EASY FOR ME", "I ENJOY DAILY EXERCISE"....
SINCLAIR

"I AM CONFIDENT AND SUCCESSFUL," "I CAN ACCOMPLISH MY GOALS"....

"COKE IS THE REAL THING."...
YOU'VE GRASPED THE CONCEPT!
7-9

SO, YOU THINK THIS NEW RADIO STATION IS THE BEST PLACE FOR OUR ADS?
YUP.

THEY HAVE AN EXCITING NEW FORMAT.
SINCLAIR

WHAT IS IT? JAZZ? CLASSICAL? R+B? C+W? A.O.R.?
READ THE FLIER!

EASY LISTENING SUBLIMINAL?
IT'S A FIRST IN THIS COUNTRY!
7-10

O.K., CRANBROOK, YOU GO CHECK OUT THIS NEW ALL-SUBLIMINAL RADIO STATION

WZMB
HIP-KNOW
103
SINCLAIR

ON AIR
EXCUSE ME....
ONE SECOND....

YOU'RE TUNED TO WZMB, WHERE YOU'LL BE SAYIN' WHAT WE'RE PLAYIN'-- NEXT UP, WE'LL HEAR THE MONTOVANNI GUITARS WITH "MY TRUE NATURE IS TRIM AND VIGOROUS."
7-11

LOTS OF STORES PLAY OUR STATION ALL DAY! WE PROVIDE PLEASANT MUSIC WITH SPECIAL SUBLIMINAL MESSAGES!

SO, ALONG WITH THE "QUITTING SMOKING" AND "BETTER LOVE LIFE" MESSAGES, I CAN USE THIS MIKE....

..TO LAY IN SPECIFIC MESSAGES FOR A PARTICULAR CLIENT WITHOUT ANYONE NOTICING! LISTEN!
SINCLAIR
7-12

ATTENTION, K MART SHOPPERS! I AM HONEST. I NEVER STEAL! SHOPLIFTING IS A CRIME!
WOW! THAT'S ENTERTAINMENT!

SO HOW WAS THE SUBLIMINAL RADIO STATION?
GREAT!

I SIGNED UP FOR OUR OWN PERSONALIZED POSITIVE AFFIRMATIONS AD!
SINCLAIR

HERE IT IS. "I LOVE AND ACCEPT MYSELF. IT'S SAFE TO BE ME"....

"I TRUST THE WAY MY LIFE IS UNFOLDING,...
"...EAT AT ALEX'S."
INSPIRING, ISN'T IT?
7-13

SO,... HOW DO YOU LIKE WORKING FOR ALEX?

OH, ALEX IS O.K.

HE'S SORT OF, YOU KNOW, POST-PSYCHEDELIC WARD CLEAVER.
SINCLAIR
7-14

MAY I HAVE A CUP OF COFFEE, PLEASE?
SURE!

HOUSE BLEND, IRISH CREAM, ENGLISH CREAM, ETHIOPIAN HARRAR, MOCHA JAVA, FRENCH ROAST, SWISS CHOCOLATE ALMOND, KENYAN BLEND, VIENNA ROAST, NICARAGUAN ORGANIC DECAF, AMARETTO, ANGELICA, HAZELNUT CREAM, HAWAIIAN KONA, VANILLA ROAST, OR PERUVIAN BREAKFAST BLEND?

HOLY COW! LOOK, MAYBE I'LL JUST HAVE A CUP OF TEA....
ORANGE PEKOE, DARJEELING, IRISH BREAKFAST, CINNAMON SPICE, LONG LIFE, INDIAN SPICE, LICORICE LEAF, ROSE HIP, PEPPERMINT, GINSENG, CHAMOMILE, RASPBERRY LEAF, CRANBERRY, OR LEMON LEAF?

GOSH... MAYBE I'LL JUST HAVE SOME WATER....
PERRIER, EVIAN, POLAND SPRINGS, CRYSTAL SPRINGS, SARATOGA, NORTHERN LIGHTS, GLACIER SPRINGS, LIME SPRITZER.........

O.K.! LOOK,... JUST GIVE ME A LITTLE CUP AND I'LL GET SOME MYSELF FROM THE TAP!
PAPER OR PLASTIC?

GEE. WHAT A GROUCH!
SINCLAIR

THAT "NEW AGE" PRODUCT SALESMAN IS HERE AGAIN.

HE'S ALWAYS COMING UP WITH SOME NEW, HOT PRODUCT FOR ALEX.
7·16
SINCLAIR

WONDER WHAT IT IS THIS TIME?

GINSENG BRAN?
THIS, MY FRIEND, IS GOING TO BE HUGE!

ENDLESS HOURS SPENT AT A COMPUTER SCREEN.... SO MANY OF US SPEND OUR LIVES AT WORK AND PLAY.....

.... LOST IN THE FLICKER OF ELECTRONS ON A PHOSPHOR AND PLASTIC SCREEN. IT'S POIGNANT AND TERRIFYING!

BUT, YOU KNOW WHAT THEY SAY....

LIFE IS TERMINAL.
DON'T YOU HAVE SOME OTHER WORK YOU COULD BE DOING?
7·17 SINCLAIR

GOOD CHOLESTEROL, BAD CHOLESTEROL, FIBER, BRAN, CALCIUM, BETA CAROTENE.... IT'S ALL A BIG MISH-MASH!

DON'T YOU THINK THIS STUFF IS ALL IN YOUR MIND?

ONLY IF YOU THINK IT IS.
7·18
SINCLAIR

WELL, YES, WE'RE TRYING TO USE PRODUCTS THAT SUPPORT RAIN FORESTS ECONOMIES,....

...AND NONE OF OUR SUSHI IS FROM JAPANESE DRIFT NETTING,.....

AND WE USE NO PRODUCTS THAT RELEASE GREENHOUSE GASES.

THIS IS THE ONLY RESTAURANT I KNOW THAT HAS A FOREIGN POLICY.
....AND MY POSITION ON GLOBAL WARMING IS WELL-KNOWN....
SINCLAIR 7-19

STEAM ROOM

STEAM ROOM
7-20
SINCLAIR

STEAM ROOM

STEAM ROOM

WELL, HOW DO YOU LIKE OUR MENU, NOW THAT YOU'VE BEEN EATING HERE FOR A WHILE?

WELL, IT'S BEEN REAL INTERESTING....

I'VE GONE THRU QUITE A CHANGE.... I'M EATING THINGS TODAY THAT SIX MONTHS AGO....

..I WOULDN'T HAVE USED FOR BAIT.
...AND ENJOYING THEM, RIGHT?
I DIDNT SAY THAT.
7-21
SINCLAIR

YOU KNOW, THERE ARE BOOKS ON HOW TO TALK TO PLANTS.

I WISH THERE WAS ONE THAT WOULD HELP ME COMMUNICATE WITH CRANBROOK!

THERE IS.

IT'S CALLED "THE SECRET LIFE OF DWEEBS".
7-23
SINCLAIR

THE USUAL? O.K.!
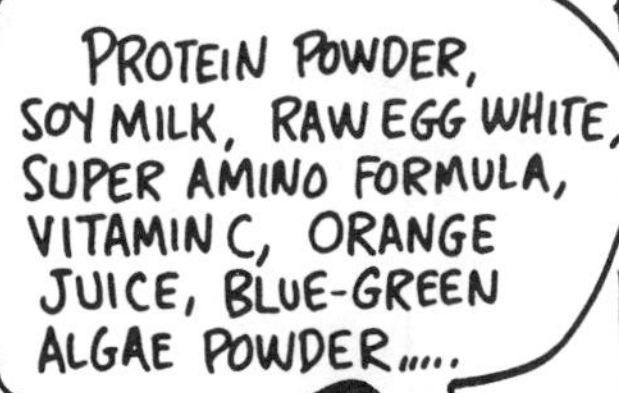
PROTEIN POWDER, SOY MILK, RAW EGG WHITE, SUPER AMINO FORMULA, VITAMIN C, ORANGE JUICE, BLUE-GREEN ALGAE POWDER.....

SINCLAIR 7-24

THERE YOU GO!

WHERE'S THE CHOCOLATE SPRINKLES?

WANT TO SEE OUR NEWEST INNOVATION? FROM NOW ON, WE'LL HAVE THE FRESHEST SALADS IN TOWN!

WE'VE DEVELOPED A "U-PICK" FRESH ORGANIC SALAD BAR. WE'VE GROWN AND LABELED THE EDIBLE WILD PLANTS IN OUR YARD.....

NOW PEOPLE CAN BURN CALORIES AS THEY PICK THEIR OWN WILD SALAD.
7-25

AND I THOUGHT A WEED EATER WAS A LAWN TOOL.
SINCLAIR

WE'VE DECIDED TO BECOME A FULL-SERVICE HEALTH FOOD CAFE.

WE'RE GOING TO OFFER BLOOD PRESSURE AND CHOLESTEROL TESTING.

WE'RE TRAINING OUR EMPLOYEES TO PERFORM SIMPLE MEDICAL PROCEDURES......
THE SCALPEL PLEASE....
7-26

WE'RE GOING TO GIVE YOU A STRESS TEST!
7-27

I'LL TAKE YOUR PULSE, THEN WE'LL SUBJECT YOU TO A STRESS TO SEE HOW IT AFFECTS YOU.

WHAT KIND OF STRESS?

HELP!
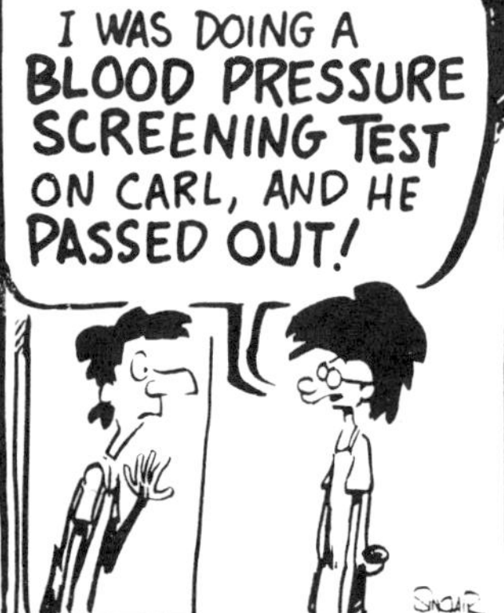
I WAS DOING A BLOOD PRESSURE SCREENING TEST ON CARL, AND HE PASSED OUT!

OVER HERE.. QUICK!

7-28
I DON'T THINK THAT BLOOD PRESSURE CUFF GOES AROUND THE NECK......
OOPS.

YOU KNOW, I THOUGHT LONG AND HARD ABOUT OPENING THIS RESTAURANT.

IT'S FUNNY,.. BUT ONE OF MY BIGGEST OBSTACLES WAS FEAR OF SUCCESS.

WELL, HANG IN THERE. I DON'T THINK YOU HAVE ANYTHING TO WORRY ABOUT.
7·30

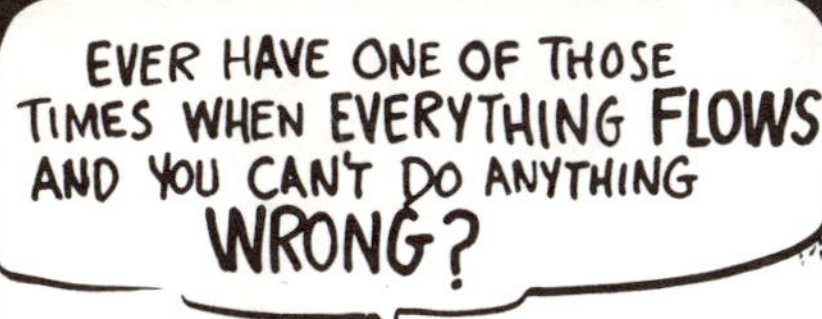
EVER HAVE ONE OF THOSE TIMES WHEN EVERYTHING FLOWS AND YOU CAN'T DO ANYTHING WRONG?

YEAH. THEY'RE CALLED "PEAK EXPERIENCES." WHY?
SINCLAIR 7·31

WELL, THIS ISN'T ONE OF THEM.

I'VE DECIDED I'M REALLY A CITIZEN OF THE FUTURE, MORE IN TUNE WITH THE POST-INDUSTRIAL ERA OF GLOBAL NEO-TRIBALISM TO COME.

OUR CURRENT LINEAR LANGUAGE HAS NO WORDS TO DESCRIBE PERSONS SUCH AS MYSELF.

I THINK "DIPSTICK" COMES PRETTY CLOSE.
I PREFER "FUTANT."
8·1

I GUESS I'LL NEVER UNDERSTAND YOU GUYS, I MEAN.....
8·2

SOMETIMES I THINK THIS WHOLE HEALTH AND WELLNESS THING....

.. IS JUST ANOTHER YUPPIE NEUROSIS!

...LIKE, HE WHO DIES WITH THE LOWEST CHOLESTEROL,... WINS!

I'M THINKING OF A BIG TV AD CAMPAIGN! FOR YOU!

I SEE A GRITTY, STEAMY STREET SCENE, A FUNKY SOUNDTRACK, 4 KIDS IN DAY-GLO SPANDEX.....

THEY'RE RAPPIN'!, THEY'RE JIVIN'! THEY'RE HIGH FIVIN'! THEY'RE MOON WALKING IN SLO-MO!...

THEY'RE EATING SEAWEED AND RICE BALLS.....
THAT'S IT!
8-3

HOW 'BOUT THIS FOR YOUR TV AD.... A BUNCH OF JOCKS AFTER A GAME....

ONE GUY SAYS, "HEY, HOW 'BOUT A BURGER AND SOME FRIES?"....
8-4

OTHER GUY SAYS, "WHAT? YOU'RE STILL EATIN' THAT GREASY KID STUFF?"

"STEP UP TO THE BROCCOLI!"
SOMETHING LIKE THAT!

I HAVE TO THINK OF AN ACTIVITY FOR THE ANNUAL COMPANY OUTING!

THE LAST FEW YEARS THEY'VE DONE ALL THESE ARDUOUS, ADVENTUROUS SORT OF THINGS TO DEVELOP GROUP IDENTITY AND BONDING.

FIRST, IT WAS RIVER RAFTING, THEN IT WAS ROCK CLIMBING, AND THEN LAST YEAR IT WAS FIRE WALKING!

SO, I NEED SOMETHING THAT'S SORT OF AN ORDEAL, THAT WE CAN ALL PARTICIPATE IN TO BUILD DISCIPLINE, TO REALLY MARK US AS A TEAM!

WHY NOT JUST BRAND 'EM ALL WITH THE COMPANY LOGO?
THAT'S GREAT! IT'S UNIQUE!! WE COULD DO THAT!!...

HEY!! WE'VE GOT TO STOP THEM! THEY'RE CUTTING THAT BEAUTIFUL OLD TREE DOWN!! THE ONE ACROSS THE STREET!

THAT'S TERRIBLE! ARE YOU SURE?
8-6
SINCLAIR

WELL, EITHER THAT, OR THEY'RE FILMING THE TEXAS CHAINSAW MASSACRE - PART NINE!
BRA-AAAK

I CAN'T LET THEM CUT THAT TREE DOWN-- I'VE GOT TO STOP THEM!
BUT HOW?
I DON'T KNOW!

TEN MINUTES LATER----
RRRING
CITY FIRE STATIO
Nº 10
8-7

YES, WE GET THINGS OUT OF TREES. WHAT DO YOU HAVE? A CAT? NO? THEN WHAT?

WELL, WE'RE NOT EXACTLY SURE!..
SINCLAIR

SIR,.. WE'VE GOT TO CUT DOWN THAT TREE. NOW, THE FIRE DEPARTMENT IS HERE TO GET YOU DOWN, IF YOU'LL JUST COME QUIETLY,....
NO! I CAN'T LET YOU!
8-8

TREES LIKE THIS ARE PRECIOUS! THEY HOLD OUR TOPSOIL, OUR HISTORY, AND OUR VALUES!
SINCLAIR

SOMEONE HAS TO DRAW A LINE! I'M PLACING MY BODY IN DEFENSE OF THE EARTH!!
?

..ALL LIFE IS CONNECTED! WE'VE ALL GOT A STAKE IN THIS!....
UH-HUH,.... WELL, THAT'S REAL NICE....
O.K., BOYS.. HOSE 'EM DOWN!

WAIT!... MY FRIEND IS TRYING TO SAVE THAT TREE! BEFORE YOU HOSE HIM OUT OF IT.... WHY DO YOU HAVE TO CUT IT DOWN?

WELL, ACTUALLY, ALL WE HAVE TO DO IS TAKE THE TOP THIRTY FEET.......

TO CLEAR THE APPROACH FOR THE SOUTH RUNWAY........
OH...., HADN'T YOU HEARD?.....
THE WHAT?

YUP. NEW AIRPORT'S GOIN' IN RIGHT HERE!
OH, NO!

WE'LL HAVE TO CUT ALL THESE TREES...

WE WERE NEVER TOLD!

GOSH, I THOUGHT EVERYONE ON SUMMIT STREET WAS NOTIFIED....

WAIT A MINUTE, THIS IS CHERRY STREET! YOU'RE ON THE WRONG SIDE OF TOWN!

IT IS? I AM? WELL, I'LL BE.....
CRANBROOK! C'MON DOWN!!

SO, ALEX, HOW CAN YOU KEEP WORKING SO HARD AT THIS WHEN CHANCES ARE YOUR CAFE IS GONNA FLOP?

SOMEBODY ONCE SAID, "WE ARE NOT CALLED MERELY TO SUCCESS, BUT TO OBEDIENCE TO OUR VISIONS!"

..AND A FEW YUCKS NOW AND THEN.
RIGHT. AND A FEW YUCKS!

THIS BOOK SAYS, TO FULLY NURTURE OUR "INNER CHILD", WE ALL HAVE TO LEARN TO BECOME OUR OWN PARENTS!

GOSH! WHAT A COMMITMENT! THIS BRINGS UP SO MANY THORNY ISSUES!

LIKE, SHOULD MY "INNER CHILD" WATCH "TWIN PEAKS"? IS HE GETTING ENOUGH "QUALITY TIME"?

GOSH! WHAT DO I TELL MY INNER CHILD ABOUT SEX AND DATING?

GOLLY, BEING YOUR OWN PARENT IS NO EASY JOB!

WHY CAN'T YOU JUST BE YOUR OWN WORST ENEMY LIKE THE REST OF US?

?

PARDON ME, BUT I COULDN'T HELP NOTICING YOU'VE PAINTED A LARGE EYE ON YOUR FOREHEAD.

YES. I'M TRYING TO BECOME MORE ATTUNED TO MY INNATE INTUITIVE ABILITY. THIS HELPS ME TO REMEMBER MY "THIRD EYE", OR PSYCHIC CENTER.

O.K., SO READ MY MIND.

YOU'RE THINKING I'M A CRETINOUS, CRACKBRAINED TWIT!
TOO EASY!

I GOT ANOTHER LETTER FROM MY RUSSIAN PEN PAL! LISTEN!....

"THE NEW FREEDOM IS EVERYWHERE! NOW I CAN PLAY MY BOOTLEGGED BARRY MANILOW TAPES ANYTIME I WANT!"
8-13
SINCLAIR

WOW! THEY REALLY ARE FREE!
I GUESS!

YOU COULD GET SHOT FOR THAT IN MY NEIGHBORHOOD!
I HEAR YA!

I JUST FINISHED CLEANING THE REFRIGERATOR AND WASHING THE WALLS.
RUB
SINCLAIR

BEFORE THAT, I POLISHED THE TABLEWARE, CLEANED THE COFFEEMAKER AND WAXED THE FLOOR!
8-14

BOY! YOU'D RATHER DO ANYTHING THAN THE MONTHLY ACCOUNTING!
YOU'RE JUST PROCRASTINATING! YOU'D BETTER GET TO IT!

IF I DIDN'T PROCRASTINATE, I'D NEVER GET ANYTHING DONE!

HEY, ALEX! DID YOU SEPARATE THE TRASH FOR RECYCLING? THE GARBAGE MEN ARE HERE!

EXCUSE ME, BUT WE'RE NOT GARBAGE MEN ANYMORE....
8-15
VERN

NOW WE'RE ADVANCED RECYCLING TECHNOLOGY EFFLUENT ENGINEERING SPECIALIST TRAINEES......
YOU MEAN.....
SINCLAIR

YUP,... WE ARE NOW A.R.T.E.E.S.T.s!
YUP.

BUT WHAT'S THE USE SEPARATING ALL THAT TRASH? WHAT CAN YOU DO WITH OLD PLASTIC, ANYWAY?

OH,.. THEY CAN MAKE LOTS OF STUFF OUT OF DISCARDED POLYSTYRENE!

CARPET PADS,.. AUTO PARTS, LAWN FURNITURE, PLASTIC PACKAGING, SWIZZLE STICKS, ROAD SURFACING MATERIAL..

EGG McMUFFINS,... VELVEETA CHEESE,....
THERE YA GO.......

CRANBROOK'S EXPERIMENTING AGAIN,...

WE'VE BEEN TRYING TO COME UP WITH AN ALTERNATIVE, BIODEGRADABLE PACKAGING FOR TAKE-OUT ORDERS,...

WHAT'S IT WRAPPED IN?
BANANA LEAVES.

YOU KNOW, IT'S TOO BAD,...

MILLET IS A STAPLE FOR MILLIONS OF THE WORLD'S PEOPLE.... BUT MOST FOLKS IN AMERICA STILL THINK OF IT AS BIRDSEED!

WHY NOT JUST HAVE ONE OF THOSE BIRDY BELLS OVER EACH TABLE AND WE CAN NIBBLE ON IT?
GO AHEAD AND MAKE FUN....

I'M DEPRESSED.
ME TOO.

DEPRESSION IS OFTEN ANGER THAT YOU'RE SUPPRESSING!

IT'S DEPRESSING TO FIND OUT HOW ANGRY YOU ARE.
YEAH. KINDA TICKS ME OFF.

O.K., CLASS! TODAY WE'RE GONNA WORK ON "ABS", "PECS", "TRAPS", "DELTS", "QUADS", "LATS"......

"GALOOTS"...

"TWITS".....
TOUCHÉ.

UH-OH. I DON'T WANT TO BUY THIS BRAND.
WHY?

IT'S BEEN IRRADIATED TO INCREASE ITS SHELF LIFE!

HOW CAN YOU TELL?

IT SAYS, "BEST IF USED BEFORE MAY 10, 2467 A.D."
OH... RIGHT.

SURGEONS, ARTISTS, AND ATHLETES ALL REPORT INSTANCES OF EXCEPTIONALLY HIGH PERFORMANCE WITH PERFECT CLARITY OF MIND!
FOOSH!
8-23

"SCIENTISTS CALL THIS, THE "FLOW STATE". I FEEL THAT EVEN AS A SIMPLE DISHWASHER, I OFTEN ACHIEVE THIS STATE OF AWARENESS.

BRAAA KAAKKAKA

IT'S KIND OF HARD TO MAINTAIN THE "FLOW STATE" WHEN YOU DROP A FORK IN THE GARBAGE DISPOSAL.

ALTHOUGH I AM A PROFESSIONAL BUSBOY AND WAITER, I PREFER TO REMAIN AN AMATEUR AT HEART......

...IN THE ORIGINAL SENSE OF THE WORD, "ONE WHO LOVES, ONE WHO CARES."
8-24

DOES THAT MEAN THE COFFEE WILL ALWAYS BE COLD AND THE TOAST BURNT?

WHO CARES?

ALEX, SOMETIMES YOU'RE TOO HARD ON CRANBROOK.
OH?

YOU KNOW HE'S JUST FOLLOWING HIS DREAMS.
YEAH...

I JUST WISH HE WOULDN'T FOLLOW THEM QUITE SO CLOSELY AT WORK......
Z....

HERE'S OUR LATEST PRODUCT, HIGH-Q BRAIN BLASTER! IT'S A BLEND OF AMINO ACIDS AND VITAL NEUROTRANSMITTERS!

IT'S SPECIALLY DESIGNED TO JOLT YOUR SYNAPSES INTO HIGHER PERFORMANCE LEVELS! YOU'LL BE ABLE TO THINK BETTER THAN EVER BEFORE!

AFTER ALL, YOUR BRAIN IS YOUR GREATEST ASSET! WHY NOT GET THE BEST OUT OF IT?
GOLLY,... I GUESS YOU'RE RIGHT!

OK., WHAT THE HECK!
GOOD CHOICE!

THIS IS A RIP-OFF, ISN'T IT?
BUT LOOK! ALREADY YOU'RE SMARTER!

WOW! I CAN'T BELIEVE IT!!

OVER THERE! I THINK THAT'S A BIG STAR!!

I THINK IT'S MY FAVORITE COUNTRY WESTERN SINGER!!!
8·27

IT IS!
YOU'RE RIGHT!

YOU'RE AL K. HALL!
YEP. AH RECKON.

IMAGINE! MY FAVORITE COUNTRY SINGER, AL K. HALL, RIGHT HERE AT ALEX'S!
YEP.

I LOVE YOUR STUFF! I LIKED YOUR VERSION OF "D-I-V-O-R-C-E" BETTER THAN TAMMY WYNETTE'S!!

YEP! AND I WROTE A SEQUEL TO IT!

IT'S CALLED T-H-E-R-A-P-Y!
8·28

COUNTRY SINGER AL K. HALL VISITS ALEX'S.....
I LOVED SO MANY OF YOUR SONGS.... LIKE "BARS, BEERS, STOGIES 'n BIMBOS"....

... AND "I MET HER AT THE LAUNDROMAT, (BUT SHE TOOK ME TO THE CLEANERS)"
WELL, TAKE A LOOK AT MY NEW CD.... IT REFLECTS A LOT OF MY PERSONAL GROWTH....
8·29

"AL K. HALL - THE EMPATHIZIN' SIDE O' ME."
YUP. I'VE MADE A LOT OF BREAKTHROUGHS LATELY.....

YUP. ALL THE NEW SONGS ON THIS C D ARE PART OF A WHOLE NEW DIRECTION FOR ME. I'M TIRED OF THE WHOLE "COWBOY-OUTLAW" SCHTICK.

"YOU UNDERMINED MY SELF-ESTEEM (BUT I CAN UNDERSTAND AND GROW THROUGH IT.)"
YEAH. THAT'S A GOOD ONE....

"I'M ADDICTED TO YOU (BUT I'M STRONGER FOR ADMITTING IT)"
"NEW AGE BLUE YODEL"

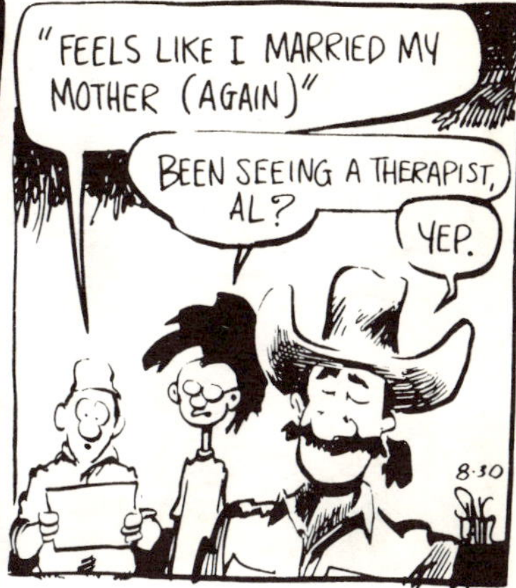
"FEELS LIKE I MARRIED MY MOTHER (AGAIN)"
BEEN SEEING A THERAPIST, AL?
YEP.
8-30

THAT COUNTRY SINGER AL K. HALL IS HERE! HE'S IN TOWN OPENING FOR THE "COWPIE JUNKIES".....

HE'S SURE GOT CARL AND CRANBROOK ENTHRALLED!
YEAH!

PROBABLY REGALING THEM WITH STORIES OF TRUCKSTOPS, BARS, HORSES, AND FAST WOMEN!
8-31

...I REMEMBER THE LAST TIME I SAW WILLIE 'n WAYLON 'n THE BOYS..... WE WUZ MEDITATIN' DOWN IN MACHU PICHU, FIXIN' TA CONTACT SOME OF THE SAUCER PEOPLE!......
WOW!

SO HOW'S YOUR CAREER THESE DAYS, AL?
A MIGHT SLOW LATELY....
....SEEMS LIKE I'M TOO OLD FOR THE TOP 40. I KEEP TRYIN' TO SNAGGLE ONE A' THOSE LATE-NIGHT TV RECORD PROMOTION DEALS... EVERYBODY SAYS I'LL BE THE NEXT SLIM WHITMAN......

..OR THE NEXT BOXCAR WILLIE, BUT IT NEVER PANS OUT.
HEY.... HANG IN THERE!
MAYBE YOU CAN BE THE NEXT "ZAMFIR- KING OF THE PANFLUTE".
AH S'POSE THAT'S WHAT IT'S COMIN' TO......
9-1

I GUESS I JUST THINK IT'S TIME FOR ALL HUMAN BEINGS TO PUT ASIDE THEIR DIFFERENCES.

AFTER ALL, WE'RE ALL JUST PASSENGERS ON SPACESHIP EARTH!

IT'S JUST THAT, SOMETIMES, I WONDER IF WE HAVEN'T BEEN BOARDED RECENTLY BY VENUSIANS.
9-3

DON'T YOU THINK SOME FOLKS GET REAL NEUROTIC ABOUT THIS HEALTHY FOOD STUFF?

I MEAN, I'VE SEEN SOME PEOPLE WHO REALLY GET CRAZY ABOUT IT!

IT'S TRUE! SCIENTISTS SAY SOME PEOPLE DO BECOME NEUROTICALLY FEARFUL ABOUT THEIR HEALTH AND THE FOOD THEY EAT.

SOME OF THESE PEOPLE ARE RISKING IRREVERSIBLE BRAN DAMAGE!
I KNEW IT!!
9-4

HEY, LOOK! I BROUGHT MY OWN DESSERT! SOME GRUBBY LITTLE JUNK-FOOD CAKES FROM THE GAS STATION! HAH!

HAVE YOU EVER CONSIDERED THAT THE FOOD YOU EAT MAY BE SUBTLY ALTERING YOUR MOODS?
MUNCH
9-5

WHAT? "HO-HO's"? DON'T MAKE ME LAUGH!

YOU MUST REALIZE THAT **PERFECTION** IS NOT THE SAME AS MERE LACK OF FLAWS.

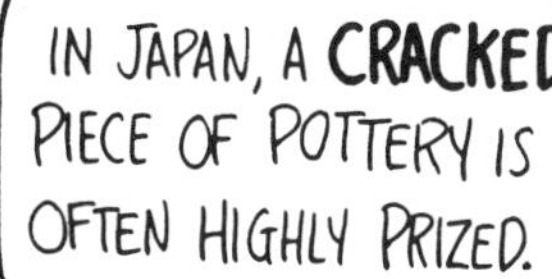
IN JAPAN, A **CRACKED** PIECE OF POTTERY IS OFTEN HIGHLY PRIZED.

WHAT'S GOING ON?
CRANBROOK SCORCHED THE PILAF.

WELL, THAT'S JUST **PERFECT!**
SEE?
9-6

I SHOULDN'T READ THESE **TRAVEL** MAGAZINES! I JUST GET DEPRESSED. I'VE NEVER BEEN **ANYWHERE**!
TRAVEL ADVENTURE

LIKE THIS ONE. IT'S ABOUT A GUY WHO PADDLED AROUND AUSTRALIA!

ISN'T HE THE ONE WHO GOT HIS LEG BITTEN OFF BY A **CROCODILE?**
9-7
YEAH. HE WRITES ABOUT IT WITH SUCH FLARE AND CONVICTION!

MAKES ME WISH I'D BEEN THERE, ALL RIGHT.....
SINCLAIR

HEY, WAITER! WHAT ARE THESE "LOUISIANA RED HOTS"?
MENU

HMMM.... LET ME SEE.....
MENU
9-8
SINCLAIR

THAT WOULD BE EITHER THE "CAJUN STYLE" BLACKENED TOFU CUTLETS.....

.....OR AN N.B.A. EXPANSION TEAM.

OBSERVE. SOME SEAWEED FROM THE AQUARIUM......

A PINCH OF GARDEN SOIL FOR THE MICRO-ORGANISMS.....

PRESTO! THE PERFECT BIOREMEDIATING DISHWASHING ENVIRONMENT! THE MICROSCOPIC CRITTERS WILL CLEAN THE DISHES LEAVING A BALANCED, PRISTINE KITCHEN WETLAND ENVIRONMENT.

WE'LL NEVER HAVE TO HAND-WASH ANOTHER DISH.
HOW LONG WILL IT TAKE?

IF IT WORKS? TWO WEEKS TOPS.

ONCE AGAIN, THE SPIRIT OF INQUIRY IS SQUASHED BY THE WHEELS OF COMMERCE.

SCIENTISTS SAY THAT WITHOUT WARM PHYSICAL CONTACT, BABIES DON'T ASSIMILATE NUTRIENTS ADEQUATELY.
9-10

THEREFORE, I WILL BE GIVING **HUGS** TO ALL CUSTOMERS AS PART OF MY REGULAR SERVICE
SINCLAIR

HOW CAN I ASSIMILATE **NUTRIENTS** IF YOU'RE MAKING ME **THROW UP?**

CRANBROOK! WAKE UP! WHAT'S **WRONG?** AREN'T YOU **THINKING?**

NOT IN THE USUAL SENSE.

I'M TRYING TO OPERATE IN SORT OF A **STREAM OF CONSCIOUSNESS!**
9-11
SINCLAIR

THAT'S NO STREAM. IT'S MORE LIKE **DRIED MUD.**

HEY, CRANBROOK! I FINALLY FIGURED OUT WHY YOU'VE BEEN HAVING SO MUCH TROUBLE HERE!

YOU'RE A **RIGHT BRAIN THINKER!** YOU'RE CREATIVE AND INTUITIVE, BUT ILLOGICAL!
9-12
SINCLAIR

YOU NEED TO USE YOUR **LEFT BRAIN,** THE LOGICAL, RATIONAL SIDE, LIKE ME!

HMMM..... I DON'T KNOW.

JUST 'CUZ YOU'RE IN YOUR **LEFT BRAIN** DOESN'T MEAN YOU'RE IN YOUR **RIGHT MIND.**

WHAT'S THE COMMOTION?
JOANNE'S HAVING ANOTHER DISCUSSION WITH CARL ABOUT HOW HE SHOULD EXPRESS HIS EMOTIONS

HOW'S IT GOING?
HE'S A TOUGH NUT TO CRACK.
9.13
SINCLAIR

GET THIS STRAIGHT! I DO NOT HAVE A SENSITIVE FEMININE SIDE!

CARL, YOU REALLY SHOULD ALLOW YOURSELF TO EXPRESS YOUR EMOTIONS
YEAH. DROP THAT SILENT MACHO IMAGE.

IT ISN'T EVEN HEALTHY
YEAH! BOTTLED UP EMOTIONS CAN MAKE YOU SICK!

LISTEN! FIRST YA START EXPRESSIN' FEELINGS, THEN YA GET ALL TOUCHY-FEELY, THEN THE NEXT THING YA KNOW.....
9.14
SINCLAIR

BANGO! YOU'RE A HAIRDRESSER!
JUST LIKE THAT?
I SEEN IT A HUNNERD TIMES!

YOU KNOW, I'M PRETTY WORRIED ABOUT THE DESTRUCTION OF THE RAIN FORESTS!

THEY'RE A BIG SOURCE OF OUR OXYGEN!
9.15
SINCLAIR

WELL, I HAVEN'T NOTICED ANY SHORTAGE.
WELL, YOU KNOW WHAT THEY SAY, THE BRAIN GOES FIRST.
YEAH...HE SOUNDS A BIT GIDDY ALREADY!

CRANBROOK, YOU SHOULD BE MORE AMBITIOUS! DON'T BE AFRAID TO STRETCH YOURSELF A LITTLE!

JUST ASK YOURSELF, "WHAT WOULD I DO IF I KNEW I COULDN'T FAIL?"

ZZZZZ......
9·17

HAH! TAKE A FEW GOOD BREATHS OF THAT FRESH MORNING AIR! IT FILLS YOU WITH LIFE FORCE!

TO THE GREEKS IT WAS "VITAL ENERGY"! TO THE CHINESE IT'S "CHI"!
9·18

TO THE JAPANESE, "KI"! TO THE INDIANS, "PRANA"!

TO THE AMERICAN'S, "HOOEY"!

THERE'S SOMETHING I DON'T GET ABOUT YOUR FOOD HERE, ALEX,...

I MEAN, I REMEMBER SEEING THIS FILM IN HIGH SCHOOL ABOUT THE FOODS THE GOVERNMENT SAYS YOU SHOULD EAT,....
YOU KNOW, THE MEAT GROUP, THE DAIRY GROUP.....

RIGHT. THE "FOUR BASIC FOOD LOBBIES."
9·19

THIS IS THE THIRD BATCH YOU'VE BURNED.

SORRY. I WAS PRACTICING WITH SOME NEW SUBLIMINAL MENTAL VISUALIZATION EXERCISES!

I'M ALWAYS LOOKING FOR NATURAL WAYS TO ALTER MY CONSCIOUSNESS!
9-20

TRY THINKING. IT WORKS FOR ME.

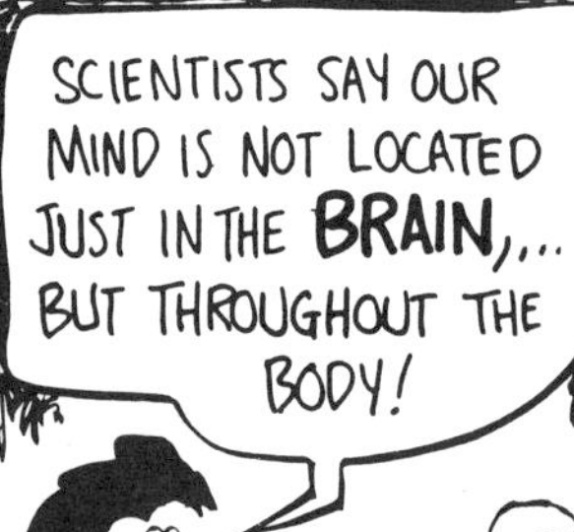
SCIENTISTS SAY OUR MIND IS NOT LOCATED JUST IN THE BRAIN,... BUT THROUGHOUT THE BODY!

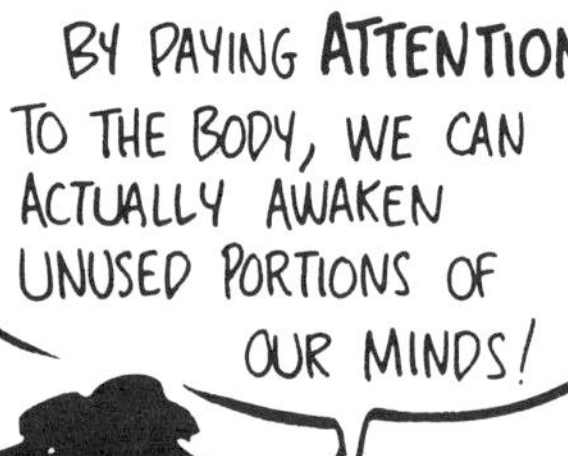
BY PAYING ATTENTION TO THE BODY, WE CAN ACTUALLY AWAKEN UNUSED PORTIONS OF OUR MINDS!

OOPS.
9-21
SLIP
CRASH!

WELL, YOU COULD PROB'LY START BY LEARNING YOUR HEAD FROM YOUR......
THAT'S ENOUGH...

THE LATEST RESEARCH SHOWS THAT RATS WHO RUN IN THE LAB GET FEWER CANCERS.
9-22

OUR NEWEST EXERCISE MACHINES ARE DESIGNED WITH THIS CONCEPT IN MIND.

READY?
LET 'ER RIP!

WE'RE FEATURING SOME CLASSIC EXAMPLES OF REGIONAL WATER SUPPLIES FROM ACROSS AMERICA.

FROM TEXAS, THE MUSKY AROMA OF VOLATILE PETROCHEMICALS.

THE DELICATE TANG OF POLYCHLORINATED BIPHENYLS FROM THE HUDSON RIVER.

FROM VERMONT, ASTRINGENCY OF ACID RAIN.

AND THIS IS OUR FINEST! CLEVELAND, 1970! STRONG ENOUGH TO MAKE GROWN MEN WEEP!

NOW, THAT'S WATER LIKE I REMEMBER IT!
WELL, HANG IN THERE! THEY'RE BRINGING IT BACK!

SINCE BIOLOGISTS SAY THAT CATTLE RANCHING IS DESTROYING THE RAIN FORESTS, SOME PEOPLE ARE RAISING **JUNGLE FAUNA** AS "RAIN FOREST FRIENDLY" LIVESTOCK.

IF IT WORKS, IT WILL GIVE CENTRAL AMERICAN FARMERS INCENTIVE TO PRESERVE THE FOREST. SO, EVEN THO' WE DON'T NORMALLY SERVE MEAT SPECIALS,......
10-8
SINCLAIR

WE SEE IT AS OUR ECOLOGICAL DUTY TO SERVE A "RAIN FOREST SPECIAL" THIS WEEK......

...BROILED PLANKED **IGUANA.**
AS USUAL I'M SPEECHLESS.

SO LET ME GET THIS **STRAIGHT,** YOU WANT TO SERVE **IGUANA MEAT...** SO CENTRAL AMERICAN FARMERS WILL HAVE INCENTIVE...

NOT TO CUT DOWN THE RAIN FOREST WHERE THE IGUANAS LIVE......
RIGHT.
GREAT. THAT'S JUST GREAT.
10-9
SINCLAIR

SO, HOW MANY DID YOU BUY?
I'M NOT SURE.

HOW MANY IGUANAS IN A CASE?
FOUR SIX-PACKS? I'M JUST GUESSING.

HEY, ALEX! YOUR SHIPMENT OF **IGUANAS** IS HERE!
GREAT!

HOW DID THEY COME? FROZEN FILLETS? SMOKED? IGUANA PATTIES?
10-10
SINCLAIR

FREEZE-DRIED? SALTED? CANNED?
WELL, AS A MATTER OF FACT.....

THEY'RE REAL **FRESH!!**
EEP! EEP! EEP! EEP!!
1 CASE
- IGUANAS -

10·11
SO HOW DO YOU COOK IGUANA?
AWP!
EEP!
1 CASE IGUANAS
I THINK YOU GOTTA BITE 'EM BETWEEN THE EYES.
NOPE. THAT'S FOR OCTOPI.
EEP!
LET'S CHECK THE INSTRUCTIONS.
EEP!
1 CASE IGUA
SINCLAIR
DO YOU HAVE A LOBSTER POT?
YOU DON'T MEAN IT!!?
EEP! PEEP!
1 CASE

HERE'S YOUR ORDER! BROILED IGUANA!
WELL, I SUPPOSE I ATE WEIRDER THINGS IN 'NAM...

I HEAR IT TASTES LIKE CHICKEN.

HEY, IT EVEN LOOKS LIKE CHICKEN!
?

GREAT DRUMSTICKS! WOW!
CRANBROOK......
10·12
SINCLAIR

WHERE ARE THE IGUANAS?
I COULDN'T BRING MYSELF TO BOIL THE LITTLE GUYS...

... SO I WENT OUT TO THE MARKET AND BOUGHT SOME CHICKEN.

10·13
SINCLAIR

O.K.....SO WHAT HAPPENED TO THE IGUANAS?

EEP!
I LIBERATED THEM.
YOU WHAT?!!?
EEP!

DID ANYONE HAPPEN TO NOTICE THAT NEW SHOP GOING IN NEXT DOOR?
ALEX'S

THEY'RE FIXING UP THAT EMPTY BUILDING.
WHAT'S IT GOING TO BE?
10·15

SOMEBODY SAID IT'S GOING TO BE ONE OF THOSE "GOURMET CHOCOLATE-CHIP COOKIE" PLACES.

OH NO! MY SECRET ADDICTION!
SINCLAIR
ALEX'S

HEL-LOOO
10·16 SINCLAIR

SO, THIS IS ALEX'S HEALTH FOOD CAFE
WELL, WELL.....

AND YOU MUST BE ALEX! I LOVE YOUR LOOK! IT'S SO,..... RIGHT!
PUMP
PUMP

EXCUSE ME, MA'AM, BUT YOU HAVE THE WRONG PERSON. I'M ALEX. ALEX RIVERSIDE.

THIS IS CRANBROOK WILSON. HE'S ONE OF OUR EMPLOYEES.
OH,..OF COURSE!
FLOP

SO PLEASED TO MEET YOU. I'M REMORA P. SILVERSPOON.
10·17

I'M OPENING THE SHOP NEXT DOOR......
KATY'S KOZY KOUNTRY KORNER KITCHEN KOOKIE NOOK!
SINCLAIR

SO HERE'S MY SHOP! KATY'S KOZY KOUNTRY KORNER KITCHEN KOOKIE NOOK!

CHOCOLATE CHUNK CHOCOLATE MINT, CHOCOLATE CHOCOLATE! CHOCOLATE CREAM! AND IT'S SO GREAT TO BE LOCATED NEXT TO A HEALTH FOOD CAFE!
?

I FEEL LIKE WE'RE PRACTICALLY IN THE SAME BUSINESS!
WHAT BUSINESS IS THAT?
SINCLAIR 10·18

GUILT.
CAN YOU ELABORATE ON THAT?

C'MON! IT'S OBVIOUS! YOUR HEALTH CAFE AND MY CHOCOLATE-CHIP COOKIE SHOP.... WE'RE BOTH IN THE GUILT BUSINESS!
10·19

PEOPLE DON'T COME TO US FOR FOOD! THEY'VE GOT FOOD! THEY WANT COMFORT, SECURITY, RELIEF FROM BOREDOM! THEY'RE DRIVEN BY PRIMAL URGES!

... SO! THEY COME TO MY PLACE AND STUFF THEMSELVES TO THE GILLS SEEKING SECURITY OR SOMETHING,.... THEN FEEL GUILTY!
© 1990 by King

.. SO THEY GO NEXT DOOR TO YOU FOR SOME HEALTHY, RIGHTEOUS SEAWEED PIE.... OR WHATEVER THE HECK YOU PEOPLE EAT!
DON'T YOU THINK THAT'S A BIT CYNICAL?
SINCLAIR

THINK OF IT! PEOPLE WILL GO TO YOUR PLACE FOR A SPROUTBURGER OR WHATEVER......

.. AND FEEL SO VIRTUOUS... THEY STOP BY MY PLACE TO REWARD THEMSELVES WITH A CHOCOLATE CHUNK DOUGH BOMB!

YOU REALLY THINK PEOPLE ARE SO SHALLOW AND PREDICTABLE?
I KNOW THEY ARE!

IT'S CYNICAL! IT'S MANIPULATIVE! ITS AMORAL.....
ITS GOOD BUSINESS!
SINCLAIR
10·20

ALEX! GLAD YOU CAME BY! I'VE MADE A NEW BREAKTHROUGH IN CHOCOLATE CHIP TECHNOLOGY!

I'M DEVELOPING A PROGRAM TO TEACH MY CUSTOMERS HOW TO USE "KATIE'S KOOKIES"...
2·4

...FOR MENTAL HEALTH, STRESS REDUCTION AND PERSONAL EMPOWERMENT. BASICALLY, WE WANT PEOPLE TO KNOW THAT IF SOMETHING IS **EATING THEM...**
"KATIE'S KOOKIES" CAN HELP THEM TO **EAT RIGHT BACK!**

MMPH.... WELL, REMORA, I'VE GOT TO ADMIT, THIS IS ONE HECK OF A COOKIE. THESE COULD BE REALLY **ADDICTIVE!**

YEAH! YOU KNOW, I'VE BEEN DOING A LOT OF READING AND RESEARCH......
2·5
WELL, I WAS READING ABOUT HOW CHOCOLATE AFFECTS THE BRAIN LIKE **HEROIN** OR **COCAINE!** SO, I DID A LITTLE EXPERIMENTING, AND.....

....WELL, I THINK I'VE BRIDGED THE GAP BETWEEN **CRACK** AND **CHOLESTEROL!**

NOW, FOR THOSE PEOPLE WHO REALLY WANT TO PAMPER THEMSELVES AND LUXURIATE IN CHOCOLATE BLISS, I'M INTRODUCING A NEW FEATURE!
2·6

EAT FOR A WHILE, THEN TAKE A BREAK, RELAX, COLLECT THEIR THOUGHTS, AND PURGE THEMSELVES IN OUR **ATHENIAN ROOM!**

...PURGE THEMSEL......
YOU'VE BUILT A **VOMITORIUM?**
IF IT WORKS OUT, I'D LIKE TO **FRANCHISE** THE THE IDEA.

I CAN'T BELIEVE YOU EXPECT PEOPLE TO PATRONIZE A **VOMITORIUM!**

WHY NOT? THERE'S AN **UNMET NEED** OUT THERE!
SINCLAIR

I PROVIDE A SECURE, ACCEPTING, DISCREET AND NON-JUDGEMENTAL ATMOSPHERE.

I MEAN, IF YOU'RE GOING TO BLOW YOUR COOKIES, SO TO SPEAK, WHAT BETTER PLACE?
OH CUTE. VERY CUTE.
2·7

YOU'RE NOT JUST CYNICAL! YOU'RE **WARPED!** THE IDEA OF RUNNING A VOMITORIUM FRANCHISE IS **DISGUSTING!**

THE WHOLE IDEA IS AN **OUTRAGE!** IT'S **SICK!** IT'S **NAUSEATING!** IT MAKES ME WANT TO.... IT MAKES ME WANT TO... UM....
2·8
SINCLAIR

WANT TO..... UH.. UMM......

WANT TO **WHAT?**
NEVER MIND!!

SO, ALEX, HOW'S BUSINESS?
NOT GREAT.

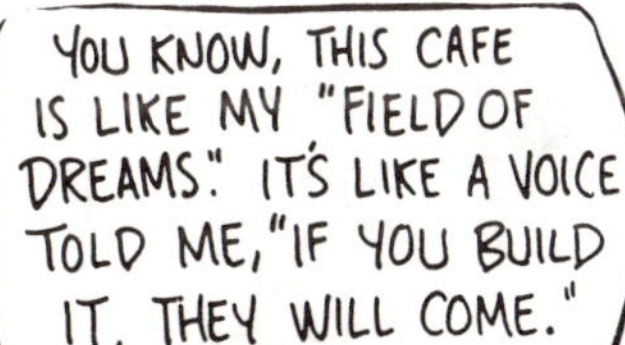
YOU KNOW, THIS CAFE IS LIKE MY "FIELD OF DREAMS." IT'S LIKE A VOICE TOLD ME, "IF YOU BUILD IT, THEY WILL COME."

SINCLAIR
2·9

SO I BUILT IT......

..AND THEY HAVE **BEAT FEET.**
SORT OF.

ALEX, I WAS READING THIS ARTICLE ABOUT COMPULSIVE WORKERS, AND I THINK YOU SHOULD LOOK AT IT.

REALLY?

THERE'S THIS QUIZ TO FIND OUT IF YOU'RE A "**WORKAHOLIC**." LET ME READ YOU SOME OF THESE QUESTIONS.

NUMBER ONE, "I ALWAYS SEEM TO BE IN A HURRY." YES OR NO?

LOOK. I DON'T HAVE TIME FOR THIS.....
THAT WOULD BE A "YES".
10·22

O.K.,.. SO THIS TEST IS SUPPOSED TO TELL IF I'M A **WORKAHOLIC**....? YOU KNOW I DON'T BELIEVE IN THESE THINGS....
JUST LISTEN....

"DO YOU FORGET BIRTHDAYS AND ANNIVERSARIES?"
NEVER.

ALWAYS. NEXT..... "MY SELF IMAGE IS DISTORTED."... YES OR NO?
NO.
10·23

YES.
HEY! WHAT'S THIS **REALLY** ALL ABOUT?

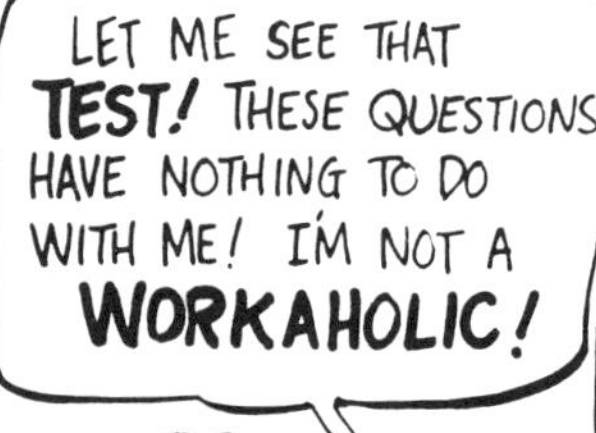
LET ME SEE THAT **TEST!** THESE QUESTIONS HAVE NOTHING TO DO WITH ME! I'M NOT A **WORKAHOLIC!**

WHAT'S THE NEXT QUESTION,.... HMMM.... "I GET IRRITATED WHEN INTERRUPTED."... YES OR NO?
10·24

SAY, ALEX....
CAN'T YOU SEE I'M BUSY?

"NO."

WHAT DO YOU THINK, CHAD? IS THERE SUCH A THING AS A "WORKAHOLIC"?

YOU'VE BEEN GOING TO "WORKAHOLICS ANONYMOUS"..... WHAT DO YOU THINK OF IT?

IT'S **GREAT** FOR **NETWORKING**! I GET A **LOT DONE** THERE!
10-25
SINCLAIR
I SEE.
YOU KNOW ME! I LIKE TO **KEEP BUSY**!

CRANBROOK, WHAT DO YOU THINK? AM I A **WORKAHOLIC**?
MAYBE. YOU KNOW, IT'S TOO BAD...
10-26

SO MANY OF US VALUE WHAT WE **DO** MORE THAN WHAT WE **ARE**. WE FORGET THAT WE'RE ALL HUMAN **BE**-INGS, NOT HUMAN **DO**-INGS!

GEE! YOU'RE **RIGHT**! THAT'S PROFOUND!

YEAH. AND THIS FROM A GUY WHOSE BIGGEST ACCOMPLISHMENT LAST WEEK WAS PICKING THE **LINT** FROM HIS BELLYBUTTON!

MAYBE I AM TOO CAUGHT UP IN MY WORK! I JUST WANT THIS BUSINESS TO SUCCEED SO MUCH!

WELL, YOU KNOW WHAT THOREAU SAID,..." MOST MEN LEAD LIVES OF QUIET DESPERATION!"
GOSH! IS THAT **IT**? IS THAT WHAT I'M DOING? I'M PROBABLY THE GUY HE WAS TALKING ABOUT! WHAT A TERRIBLE THOUGHT!
SINCLAIR

THOREAU PROBABLY WOULDN'T EVEN **LIKE** ME!
CAREFUL. NOW YOU'RE VEERING INTO "QUIET PARANOIA."
10-27

AH! SUCH AROMA! SUCH COLOR!

IT'S SAID THAT COOKING IS THE HIGHEST ART, SINCE IT DETERMINES OUR HEALTH AND QUALITY OF LIFE!

THE MODERN CHEF COMBINES TRADITION WITH ORIGINALITY.
SZZ ZZZ
COOK BOOK

HEY, CARL! I JUST INVENTED A WHOLE NEW DISH!
SIZZLE

CHECK IT OUT! WHAT DO YOU THINK OF MY "STIR FRY SUPREMO"?

OH. FOR A MINUTE THERE, I THOUGHT IT WAS "YOUR BRAIN ON DRUGS."
FIZZLE
SIZZLE

THIS IS MY COUSIN BART!
HI!
10·29
BART'S A **FOOD DESIGNER!** HE INVENTS THOSE TASTY SNACKS YOU CAN GET AT GAS STATIONS AND PARTY STORES.

YES, MY LATEST IS "BETTY CROCKA'S TOAST'EM CHEEZY GUTTERSNAPS"!
SINCLAIR

WOW!
YES! AND NOW NEW MICROWAVABLE GUTTERSNAPS!

AS A FOOD TECHNOLOGIST, BART HERE INVENTS NEW TYPES OF CONVENIENCE FOODS!
NEAT!... UH.... HERE'S YOUR SALAD!

HMMM... THIS COULD BE FABRICATED FROM HYDROLIZED VEGETABLE PROTEIN.....

SINCLAIR 10·30

....A LITTLE KEVLAR, GLUTAMATE, AND GL-70....

SAY!.... YOU MAY HAVE SOMETHING HERE...!
WE LIKE 'EM

STEP RIGHT IN! SIT DOWN! YOU CAME TO THE RIGHT INVESTMENT SERVICE!

10·31

WE'VE GOT SOMETHING FOR EVERYONE! BONDS! FUNDS! UTILITY STOCKS! BLUE CHIPPERS! ANNUITIES! WE'VE GOT THE PLAN FOR YOU!
ACTUALLY, I WAS THINKING OF MAKING SOME **ETHICAL INVESTMENTS!**

HEY, **TED!** WE GOT ANYTHING **ETHICAL?**
SURE!
THERE YOU GO!
SINCLAIR

I'LL LET YOU SPEAK TO OUR **ETHICAL INVESTMENT EXPERT!**

I'M SURE WE CAN FIND THE RIGHT ETHICAL INVESTMENT PLAN FOR YOU.

WE WANT ALL OUR CUSTOMERS TO GET GOOD RETURNS ON THEIR **PRINCIPLES!**
SINCLAIR

IN FACT, I THINK I CAN SAY IT'S REALISTIC THAT WE CAN **DOUBLE** YOUR **MORALITY** IN 5 YEARS!!
WOW!
11-1

IS THIS **ALEX RIVERSIDE?** YES, MR. RIVERSIDE, THIS IS THE INVESTMENT AGENCY! I'VE SET UP AN EXCELLENT **ETHICAL INVESTMENT** STRATEGY FOR YOU!

YOU WANTED A SMALL BUSINESS, NO SEXISM, NO OIL COMPANIES, NO BIG POLLUTERS, NO TOBACCO COMPANIES, NO DEFENSE CONTRACTORS, NO SOUTH AFRICAN TIES..... SO I'VE LOCKED YOU IN FOR **6 MONTHS...**

...WITH A HALF INTEREST IN SOMETHING CALLED "KATY'S KOZY KOUNTRY KORNERS KITCHEN KOOKIE NOOK"!
SINCLAIR 11-2

WHAT'S WITH ALEX?
I DON'T KNOW! HE JUST DROPPED THE PHONE AND RAN OUT SCREAMING!

OK, LET ME GET THIS STRAIGHT... ALEX'S INVESTMENT COUNSELOR PUT HIS MONEY INTO THE COOKIE LADY'S SHOP NEXT DOOR?
FOR 6 MONTHS!

BUT ALEX **HATES** THE COOKIE LADY!
SHE'S RUTHLESS AND UNSCRUPULOUS! ALEX IS TERRIBLY DEPRESSED!

WHERE IS HE NOW?
HE'S WORKING UP FRONT, TRYING TO FORGET IT ALL....

WHERE'S MY BUDDY?
AAUGH!

WELL, THIS IS ALL VERY INTERESTING, REMORA, BUT IT'S PURELY AN ACCIDENT THAT MY MONEY WAS INVESTED HERE, AND I DON'T AGREE WITH WHAT YOU DO HERE.

DON'T SAY THAT! YOU'RE IMPOSING **LIMITATIONS** ON YOURSELF.

SORRY, BUT I DON'T AGREE WITH YOUR BUSINESS PHILOSOPHY.... I DON'T WANT TO PUT MY ENERGY INTO SOMETHING I DON'T BELIEVE IN!

I JUST DON'T THINK I CAN LIVE A **LIE**!
BUT THAT'S JUST **IT**! THAT'S THE **WONDERFUL** THING! YOU **CAN**! **YOU CAN!**
11·5
SINCLAIR

SINCE WE'RE **PARTNERS** NOW, YOU MIGHT WANT TO STUDY SOME BOOKS IN MY **BUSINESS** LIBRARY.

HERE'S MY OLD FAVORITE, "HOW TO SWIM WITH THE SHARKS WITHOUT BEING EATEN!"
NOW THERE'S A NEW ONE BY THE SAME GUY.
OH? WHAT'S IT CALLED?

"HOW TO SLITHER WITH THE SNAKES WITHOUT GETTING RATTLED."
I KNEW THAT. HOW DID I KNOW THAT?
11·6
SINCLAIR

LOOK, WE HAVE A **FUNDAMENTAL** CONFLICT. I THINK EATING SHOULD BE A **GUILT-FREE ACTIVITY**!
OH, NO! **GUILT IS GOOD!**
GUILT IS **RIGHT**! GUILT IS **NATURAL**! **GUILT SELLS COOKIES**!
SINCLAIR

HERE AT "KATY'S KOOKIES" GUILT IS ONE OF OUR SECRET INGREDIENTS!
11·7
WE LIKE TO SAY THE GUILT GOES RIGHT IN WITH THE **SUGAR**!

GEE, JUST LIKE **MOM'S**!

LET ME SHOW YOU ANOTHER OF MY SECRET SUBLIMINAL SALES TECHNIQUES!
11·8
SINCLAIR

SPECIAL SCENTS.... DESIGNED TO INFLUENCE THE COOKIE CUSTOMER'S UNCONSCIOUS MIND!
PWEET PWEET

SO WHAT'S THE SMELL? CHOCOLATE, I SUPPOSE?

NOPE. THE SWEAT OF RUTTING BULLS.
POOT POOT

LOOK, REMORA, WE CAN BE FRIENDS, BUT I DON'T AGREE WITH YOUR WAY OF DOING BUSINESS. IT'S CYNICAL AND DISHONEST.

BOY! YOU WON'T GET FAR IN THE WORLD WITH THAT ATTITUDE!

OH YEAH? WELL, AT LEAST I CAN LIVE WITH MY CONSCIENCE!

C'MON, LIGHTEN UP, MAN! THIS IS THE EIGHTIES!
NO IT'S NOT!
OH, YEAH! WELL, YOU KNOW WHAT I MEAN!
11·9
SINCLAIR

WELL, I GUESS THE CHOCOLATE-CHIP COOKIE LADY MADE A POOR IMPRESSION ON ALEX! I'VE NEVER SEEN HIM SO UPSET!

I GOT THE IMPRESSION SHE'S NOT GOING TO BE WELCOME AROUND HERE.
WELL, I CAN'T SAY I'M SORRY ABOUT THAT.

HE MADE IT PRETTY CLEAR HE DIDN'T WANT ANY OF US TO GIVE HER ANY BUSINESS!
11·10
SINCLAIR

I GUESS HE'D BE UPSET IF HE KNEW ABOUT MY WEAKNESS FOR CHOCOLATE-CHIP COOKIES!
MUNCH!

WELL, WE'VE FINISHED YOUR PSYCHOLOGICAL HEALTH PROFILE ANALYSIS.

A LOT OF HEALTH CLUBS ARE DOING THIS THESE DAYS TO HELP CLIENTS WITH THEIR SPECIFIC PSYCHOPHYSICAL PROBLEMS.

SO WHAT DOES MINE LOOK LIKE?
11-12

WELL, TO PUT IT PLAINLY, IT APPEARS AS THOUGH YOU'RE A WIMP, TRAPPED IN THE BODY OF A GEEK!
GEE! THAT EXPLAINS SO MUCH!

SO, YOU DID A COMPLETE PSYCHOPHYSICAL PROFILE WORKUP ON ME......
11-13

..AND IT TURNS OUT I'M A WIMP?
IN LAYMAN'S TERMS, YES.

SINCLAIR

MAYBE I'M JUST MORE IN TOUCH WITH MY FEMININE SIDE.
NOPE. WE SCREENED FOR THAT.

URK!
CRICK!

MY BACK! SOMETHING POPPED!
SINCLAIR 11-14

PAY ATTENTION TO YOUR BODY! WHAT IS IT SAYING?

RIGHT NOW IT'S SAYING,.... SOMEBODY SHOOT ME!

WELL, MR. RIVERSIDE, ALL I CAN REALLY DO FOR YOUR BACK PAIN, SINCE YOU DON'T WANT SURGERY, IS PRESCRIBE SOME DRUGS FOR PAIN!

BUT REMEMBER, WHEN YOU TAKE THESE, YOU WON'T BE ABLE DRIVE, WORK, READ, WALK, TALK, EAT OR SLEEP.
11·15
SINCLAIR

WELL, WHAT DO YOUR OTHER PATIENTS DO, THEN?

OH, MOSTLY SIT, WATCH TV AND DROOL.

DOC.... I CAN'T BELIEVE DRUGS ARE THE ONLY WAY TO HANDLE MY BACK PAIN! ISN'T THERE AN ALTERNATIVE? SOMETHING I CAN DO MYSELF?

WELL, IT'S IMPRACTICAL. YOU'D HAVE TO CHANGE YOUR LIFE, UNLEARN BAD HABITS.... NOBODY WANTS TO DO THAT, SO, FRANKLY, I'VE NEVER EVEN LOOKED INTO IT.

11·16
SINCLAIR

BUT, DOC, PEOPLE CAN CHANGE...... CAN'T THEY?
NO RESPONSIBLE MEDICAL AUTHORITY BELIEVES THAT.

FACE IT! PEOPLE WILL NEVER CHANGE THEIR HEALTH HABITS. THEY'D MUCH RATHER WAIT TILL SOMETHING BREAKS DOWN, THEN RUN TO A DOCTOR FOR A MAGIC POTION OR PILL.

YOU KNOW, A MAJOR MEDICAL SCHOOL DID A SURVEY ON LIFESTYLE CHANGE.

THEY FOUND THAT MOST PEOPLE ARE RIGID, INFLEXIBLE, NARROW-MINDED AND RESISTANT TO MEANINGUL CHANGE!
11·17
SINCLAIR

REALLY? WHO DID THEY SURVEY?
UH,.. WELL, MEDICAL STUDENTS, OF COURSE,... WHY?

SO, I HEARD YOU WERE LOOKING FOR A DIFFERENT APPROACH TO HELP YOUR BACK PAIN.
HEY, I'LL TRY ANYTHING!
WELL, I HEARD ABOUT THIS INDIAN MEDICINE MAN,... HE HOLDS SWEAT LODGE CEREMONIES EVERY WEEK! MAYBE HE COULD HELP YOU!
11-19
SINCLAIR
I'M GAME! WHERE DOES HE DO IT?
FOLLOW ME!
STEAM ROOM

SEEKING HELP FOR HIS BAD BACK, ALEX ATTENDS THE SWEAT LODGE CEREMONY OF LITTLE EAGLE, A NATIVE AMERICAN MEDICINE MAN....
WELCOME, BROTHER! I HOPE WE CAN BE OF HELP.
IF YOU'RE SINCERE, THE MEDICINE WAY CAN BE VERY HEALING. I GET A LOT OF PEOPLE WHO AREN'T VERY SERIOUS, THOUGH.
REALLY?
OH, YES!

I CALL THEM "POTTAWATTAMIE WANNABEES."
11-20

YES, THE SWEAT LODGE CEREMONY IS VERY ANCIENT AMONG MY PEOPLE. THE CHIPPEWA TRIBE, THE APACHE TRIBE,...
THE NAVAHO TRIBE, THE CHEROKEE TRIBE,...
I'VE HEARD THERE'S NOW ALSO A HOT TUB CEREMONY.
YOU'RE THINKING OF THE "MALIBU TRIBE."
11-21
SINCLAIR

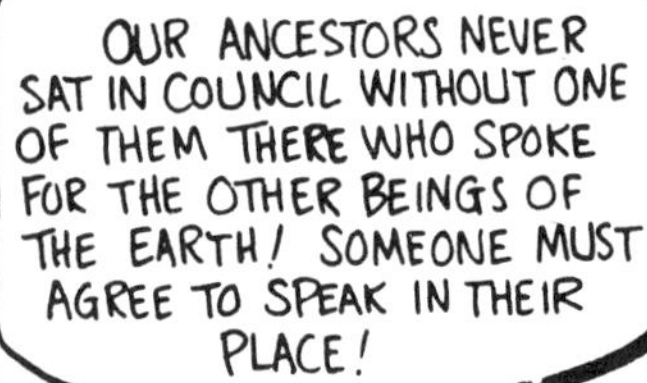
OUR ANCESTORS NEVER SAT IN COUNCIL WITHOUT ONE OF THEM THERE WHO SPOKE FOR THE OTHER BEINGS OF THE EARTH! SOMEONE MUST AGREE TO SPEAK IN THEIR PLACE!

NOW I ASK, WHO AMONG US WILL SPEAK FOR **WOLF?**

ARF!
THANK YOU AND WELCOME, BROTHER.

SO, LITTLE EAGLE HOW LONG HAVE YOU BEEN DOING YOUR **SWEAT LODGE** CEREMONY HERE AT THE HEALTH CLUB.

A FEW MONTHS. BUT WE'RE BUILDING A TRADITIONAL LODGE OUT ON THE RESERVATION. WE'RE REALLY WORKING ON REBUILDING OUR **ANCIENT TRADITIONS!**

YOU SHOULD COME ON OUT SOMETIME.
WHERE IS IT?

IT'S EASY TO FIND!..... RIGHT BEHIND THE **CASINO!**

SO YOU KNOW WHAT YOU NEED TO DO! IF YOU WANT TO MAINTAIN HEALTH, YOU MUST **LISTEN** TO YOUR BODY.

WASN'T IT A GREAT MEDICINE MAN WHO SAID, "LET ME HEAR YOUR BODY TALK, YOUR BODY TALK, LET ME HEAR YOUR BODY TALK"?

GEE, WHO WAS IT, CHIEF SEATTLE? BLACK ELK? CRAZY HORSE?

ACTUALLY, I THINK THAT WAS **OLIVIA NEWTON-JOHN.**
OH.

WHAT A GREAT DAY!

YOU KNOW, ON A DAY LIKE THIS, I FEEL..... A ONENESS WITH ALL LIFE!

WELL, EXCEPT FOR ICKY WORMS AND SPIDERS.
OF COURSE!
12·3

SO, ALEX, HAS THE HEALTH DEPARTMENT EVER COME IN HERE?
OH YEAH! A FEW TIMES!

I'VE MET ALL THE REGULATIONS AND I'M THINKING OF ADDING SOME EXTRA SAFETY FEATURES.
LIKE WHAT?

CRASH
OUCH!
12·4

WELL, LIKE HAVING SOME EMPLOYEES EQUIPPED WITH AIR BAGS!

HEY! LET'S KNOCK OFF EARLY AND TAKE IN A FILM!
GREAT! WHAT'S ON?

WELL, LET'S SEE. WHAT KIND OF MOOD ARE YOU IN?

DO YOU WANT TO BE "SHATTERED"?... "TERRIFIED"?... "SHOCKED"?...
12·5

...OR JUST BE "BLOWN OUT OF THE BACK OF THE THEATER"?
GEE..... SO HARD TO DECIDE...

YOU KNOW, ALEX GETS SO MAD AT ME SOMETIMES, I WORRY ABOUT HIM.

HE MAY BE WHAT DOCTORS CALL A "HOT REACTOR". IT'S BAD FOR HIS HEALTH.

YOU MEAN HE MIGHT GET HIGH BLOOD PRESSURE?
I WAS THINKING MORE OF SPONTANEOUS HUMAN COMBUSTION!
CRANBROOK!
OOPS, GOTTA GO!
SINCLAIR 12·6

I JUST WISH PEOPLE COULD ALL APPRECIATE THE NATURAL WORLD AND REALIZE WE HAVE TO LIVE IN HARMONY WITH IT!

THERE YOU GO SERMONIZING AGAIN!

THIS IS THE 20th CENTURY! YOU CAN'T EXPECT US TO ALL BE TREE HUGGERS AND POSIE PICKERS!

I THINK CARL'S SAYING YOU'RE ESPOUSING "ADAM AND EVE" VALUES IN A "KEN AND BARBIE" WORLD.
RIGHT!
12·7

THE SOUP OF THE DAY IS ONION LENTIL, THE SALAD OF THE DAY IS SPINACH WITH PUMPKIN SEEDS, THE MUFFIN OF THE DAY IS HONEY-BRAN,....

THE BEAN OF THE DAY IS ANASAZI, THE GRAIN OF THE DAY IS BARLEY, THE....
OK., OK.! I'LL TAKE THE USUAL.

PEANUT BUTTER AND JELLY? COMIN' UP!
THANKS.... SIGH
ZIP

12·8
.... ANOTHER DAY IN THE GARBANZO GULAG.

YOU KNOW, PEOPLE TALK ABOUT THE **BRAZILIAN RAIN FOREST...**

I MEAN, ONE GUY'S "ANCIENT FOREST ECOSYSTEM" IS ANOTHER GUY'S **TOILET PAPER!**

NOTHING DISTURBS THE WARRIOR'S PERFECT CALM. THE PETTY ANNOYANCES OF LIFE NEVER UPSET HIM.

SINCLAIR

THIS PLACE IS SO DISORGANIZED!!

DON'T WORRY! A CERTAIN CALCULATED DISORGANIZATION IS GOOD FOR CREATIVITY!

WE MUST RISK DISORDER IF WE HOPE TO FIND SOMETHING NEW!
12·13

BUT I CAN'T EVEN FIND A SILLY OLD POTATO PEELER!

WHATCHA READIN' NOW?
12·14

THIS IS A THEORY OF "DEEP ECOLOGY"!

IT SAYS WE HAVE TO LEARN TO "THINK LIKE A MOUNTAIN."

SOUNDS LIKE A TALL ORDER, 'SPECIALLY SINCE YOU'RE STARTING WITH THE CLASSIC MOLEHILL.

YOU KNOW, THE WORLD IS A CONFUSING PLACE.

IT SEEMS AS THOUGH EACH MAN VIEWS REALITY THROUGH HIS OWN PECULIAR FILTER!

WOULD YOU SAY YOURS IS "REGULAR" OR "MENTHOL"?
12·15

IT WAS KINDA WEIRD TO SPEND A NIGHT WITHOUT TV
I STARTED TO HEAR THINGS GOING ON IN MY OWN HEAD!
YOU MEAN, THOUGHTS AND STUFF?
YEAH, AND AFTER A WHILE... IT GOT REAL QUIET, LIKE, IT WAS JUST ME... BY MYSELF.....
WOW!
WHAT YOU HAD IS AN EXPERIENCE MANY COUCH POTATOES HAVE REPORTED UNDER SIMILAR CIRCUMSTANCES....
SOME WRITERS REFER TO IT AS A "NEAR LIFE" EXPERIENCE!
WELL, WHATEVER YA CALL IT, IT WAS HEAVY-DUTY!
I'M HIP!

LISTEN, I KNOW YOU'VE BEEN LETTING GROUPS USE YOUR SPACE UPSTAIRS,...
KATY'S KOZY KOUNTRY KORNERS KITCHEN KOOKIE NOOK
12·17

I'VE CONTACTED A "12 STEP" GROUP I THINK WE SHOULD SUPPORT!

CHOCOHOLICS ANONYMOUS?

BUT THEY,... THAT WOULD MEAN... IF THEY COME THEN,...

YOU'RE DESPICABLE.
WHY? THESE PEOPLE ARE MY BEST CUSTOMERS!
CHOCOLATE CHIP
CHOCOLATE CHUNK
CHOCOLATE WONK
CHOCOLATE BLOCK
SINCLAIR

REMORA, THE CHOCOLATE COOKIE LADY, ADDRESSES THE FIRST MEETING OF "CHOCOHOLICS ANONYMOUS"....
I WANT YOU ALL TO KNOW,...

THAT I UNDERSTAND YOUR STRUGGLE AND I ADMIRE YOUR COURAGE! I'M INVITING YOU ALL TO A SPECIAL VIDEO PRESENTATION AT MY COOKIE SHOP NEXT DOOR,....

"KNOW YOUR ENEMY: A HISTORY OF CHOCOLATE"....
12·18

...FROM THE ACCLAIMED PBS SERIES...... REFRESHMENTS AND SNACKS WILL BE SERVED!
? ? ?

FINALLY, I WANT YOU TO KNOW THAT WE AT "KATY'S KOOKIES" ARE BEHIND YOU IN YOUR FIGHT TO KICK THE CHOCOLATE HABIT!
12·19

BUT,... IF IT GETS TO BE TOO MUCH, IF YOU SHOULD SLIP,... WE'LL BE THERE TO SUPPORT YOU.

REMEMBER, WE'LL UNDERSTAND AND WE'LL STICK BY YOU!....

... AND IT'LL BE OUR LITTLE SECRET!
SIGH.

CHAD, ARE YOU GIVING REMORA MARKETING ADVICE?
NO. WHY?

SHE'S PUSHING HER COOKIES ONTO HELPLESS CHOCOHOLICS WHO PROBABLY DON'T REALIZE WHAT CHOLESTEROL BOMBS THOSE THINGS ARE!

THAT'S NOT TRUE! PEOPLE LIKE TO KNOW OUR COOKIES ARE RICH! IT MAKES THEM FEEL A LITTLE RECKLESS, A LITTLE ADVENTUROUS!
12-20

WE'RE EVEN APPLYING TO THE ATTORNEY GENERAL TO GET A WARNING LABEL!
SEE? SHE DOESN'T NEED ANY HELP FROM ME!

HOW CAN YOU TAKE ADVANTAGE OF THESE CHOCOLATE ADDICTS LIKE THIS?
HEY! I'M GIVING THEM WHAT THEY REALLY WANT!

I'M NOT SO SURE ABOUT THAT!
HEY, YOU'RE A BUSINESSMAN!...

SO?

WELL, YOU KNOW ABOUT MARKETING! I GOTTA MAKE A LIVING!

ARE YOU TRYING TO MAKE A LIVING, OR JUST A KILLING?
THAT'S SO CUTE! YOU DIDN'T MAKE THAT UP, DID YOU?
12-21

YOU GOTTA HAND IT TO CRANBROOK.
12-22

IF NOTHING ELSE, HE'S GOT A SENSE OF STYLE. HIS "LOOK" REALLY FITS HIS PERSONALITY.

I DON'T KNOW.

I THINK HE COULDA JUST SETTLED ON A LITTLE BEANIE WITH A PROPELLER.

HEY, GUYS! WAIT'LL YOU HEAR! WE'VE GOT SOMETHING TERRIFIC HAPPENING THIS WEEK!

A DOLPHIN SWIM! THIS WEEK, IN OUR POOL, YOU CAN SWIM WITH A REAL DOLPHIN!
WOW!

A CHANCE TO REALLY TRY SOME INTERSPECIES COMMUNICATION!
RIGHT! YOU GUYS UP FOR IT?
SINCLAIR
I DON'T KNOW. I FEEL LIKE I'VE HAD ALL THE INTERSPECIES CONTACT I CAN STAND RIGHT HERE!
12·24

IN A MOMENT, WE WILL BEGIN YOUR "DOLPHIN EXPERIENCE." I MUST TELL YOU HOW LUCKY WE ALL ARE TO HAVE "FLIPPY" WITH US THIS WEEK. WE'VE FILLED THE POOL WITH SALT WATER...

... AND PROVIDED EVERYTHING YOU'LL NEED FOR A HIGH QUALITY, CONSCIOUSNESS-RAISING EXPERIENCE WITH NATURE'S MOST INTELLIGENT CREATURE!

REMEMBER, "FLIPPY" LOVES PEOPLE AND WANTS TO HAVE FUN WITH YOU, TOO! HE ESPECIALLY LIKES TO PLAY "CATCH" WITH HIS LITTLE RED BALL,.....
SINCLAIR

...AND GET LITTLE TREATS FROM HIS BOX OF "DOLPHIN CHOW."
E-EESH,..... THIS GUY IS TALKIN' THROUGH HIS BLOWHOLE!
12·25

LOOK! THERE HE IS! SUCH PERFECT PLAYFULNESS AND SIMPLICITY!

I CAN'T WAIT FOR MY TURN TO JUMP IN WITH "FLIPPY"!

I WONDER WHAT HE THINKS OF ALL US HUMANS LOOKING DOWN AT HIM?
12·26

HE PROBABLY LOOKS AT US AS SOME KIND OF GODS OR SOMETHING!
WELL,... HERE COME THE YOKELS.....

I FEEL LIKE I'M REALLY TOUCHING ONE OF LIFE'S PROFOUND MYSTERIES! I'M IN AWE OF THE VAST ENIGMA OF OUR PLANET'S LIFE PROCESS!

HE TALKS! HE REALLY TALKS!
IS THAT SURPRISING? MY BRAIN'S BIGGER THAN YOURS, Y'KNOW.
WELL, IF YOUR NAME'S NOT FLIPPY, WHAT IS IT?
MY DOLPHIN NAME IS SORT OF A SQUEAK YOU COULDN'T HEAR.
BUT I'M TRYING TO DECIDE ON A HUMAN-TYPE NAME
LIKE WHAT?
I'M CONSIDERING "DUKE" OR "CLINT." WHAT DO YOU THINK?
12-31

SO WHAT WERE YOU DOING FOR THE NAVY?
IT'S TOP SECRET!

THEY'RE TRYING TO TRAIN SQUADS OF ELITE DOLPHIN SPECIAL FORCES TEAMS FOR SOPHISTICATED, DANGEROUS, COVERT ACTIVITIES.

NAVY DOLPHINS! GEE, I'VE HEARD OF NAVY "SEALS,"......
WIMPS!..... WIMPS AND WOOSIES!.... ....COMPARED TO MY OUTFIT!
1-1

SO THE NAVY TAUGHT YOU TO TALK?
I'LL NEVER FORGIVE THEM FOR IT!
WHY?

WHY? NOW I'VE GOT YOUR WHOLE SICKO CULTURE RATTLING AROUND INSIDE MY HEAD! I USED TO,.. JUST SWIM,.... JUST EAT,.... JUST SLEEP,.... JUST BE! NOW I HEAR ALL THESE LITTLE VOICES!

COMMERCIALS! JINGLES! SLOGANS! POP SONGS!.... LITTLE VOICES ASKING STUFF LIKE,.... AM I HAPPY? OR,.. OR..
...AM I HAVING FUN YET?
EXACTLY!
1-2

SO WHY ARE YOU RUNNING FROM THE NAVY?
LOTSA REASONS.

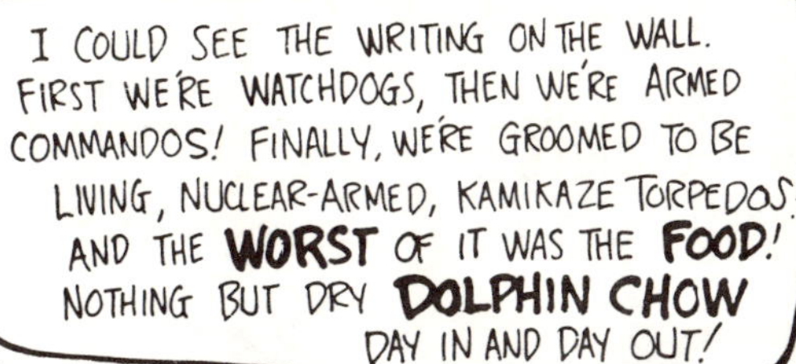
I COULD SEE THE WRITING ON THE WALL. FIRST WE'RE WATCHDOGS, THEN WE'RE ARMED COMMANDOS! FINALLY, WE'RE GROOMED TO BE LIVING, NUCLEAR-ARMED, KAMIKAZE TORPEDOS! AND THE **WORST** OF IT WAS THE **FOOD**! NOTHING BUT DRY **DOLPHIN CHOW** DAY IN AND DAY OUT!

1·3

WHAT'S SO BAD ABOUT THAT?
TUNA FLAVOR? I MEAN, HOW **CRASS** CAN YOU BE?

THERE'S STILL SO MANY HUMAN CONCEPTS I DON'T GET. LIKE,.. **WORK**,... **AUTHORITY**,.... **FEAR**,.... AND ESPECIALLY,..... **LYING**! THAT REALLY IS A MYSTERY TO ME!

WHY WOULD YOU SAY THINGS THAT AREN'T REAL? I MEAN, IT SEEMS SO SILLY. SO SAD! SUCH A WASTE!
1·4

UH-OH! HERE COMES ROIDS! DOES HE KNOW ABOUT YOU?
NO! AND DON'T TELL HIM!
TELL HIM **ANYTHING!** MAKE UP A STORY! FEED HIM ANY OLD LINE! DON'T LET HIM KNOW ABOUT ME!

WAIT!..... I'M DOING IT, AREN'T I?.....
IT'S EASY TO FALL INTO......

HEY! YOU GUYS LOOK PRETTY SERIOUS OVER HERE! ALMOST LIKE YOU'RE HAVING A HEAVY **CONVERSATION** WITH FLIPPY! HA!
?

NOW IT'S TIME FOR ANYONE THAT WANTS THEIR PICTURE TAKEN WITH FLIPPY......
HIS NAME ISN'T.....
UH-OH!

1·5
FLIP!
SPOOSH!

GEE, IT'S ALMOST LIKE LIKE HE'S **LAUGHING** AT ME.
EERIE, ISN'T IT?
HA HA HA HA HA HA HA

HOW DID I LET YOU GET ME INTO THIS?
1·7

HERE I AM HAVING A CONVERSATION WITH A BIG, BLUE DOLPHIN! THIS IS NOT POSSIBLE!! IT JUST DOESN'T MAKE SENSE!

IT'S GOTTA BE SOME KINDA GIMMICK! SOME KINDA TRICK! THINGS LIKE THIS DON'T HAPPEN! AT LEAST, NOT TO ME!
?

I'M NOT GONNA LET THIS PUSH ME OVER THE EDGE!
TOO LATE!

YOU'VE BLOWN CARL'S REALITY CONCEPT TO SMITHEREENS!
THIS CAN'T BE HAPPENING TO ME.....

IT ALL SEEMS UNREAL SOMEHOW.......

WHAT IF IT GETS OUT THAT I WAS TALKING TO A FISH?
1·8

I'M NOT A FISH..... I'M A MAMMAL!
THAT'S WORSE!

DON'T WORRY, CARL. YOU CAN JUST BE AN AVERAGE GUY THAT TALKS TO DOLPHINS!
AVERAGE GUYS DO NOT TALK TO DOLPHINS!
I LIKE BEING AVERAGE! ALL MY LIFE I'VE BEEN AVERAGE! ORDINARY! TYPICAL! A MIDDLE AMERICAN! I LIKE IT THAT WAY! I WANT TO STAY THAT WAY!!

DOESN'T THE WORD NORMAL MEAN ANYTHING TO YOU?

IT'S A SETTING ON A WASHING MACHINE, ISN'T IT?
I DON'T THINK YOU KNOW WHAT THIS MEANS TO ME.......
1·9

LOOK PAL, I'VE GOT NOTHIN' AGAINST YOU, BUT I'VE GOTTA GET OUTTA HERE! TALKING WITH DOLPHINS JUST ISN'T **ME**, YOU KNOW?

WHAT'LL I RUN INTO NEXT? THE WICKED WITCH OF THE WEST? THE SUGARPLUM FAIRY!?

PEOPLE WILL SAY, "HEY, CARL! WHAT'D YOU SEE THIS WEEK? **ELVES? DWARVES? TROLLS? GREMLINS?**

HEY, I JUST **TALKED** TO THE GUY,... I DIDN'T GRANT HIM THREE **WISHES**, FOR GOSH SAKES.
HE'S QUITE SENSITIVE ABOUT THIS.
1·10

I THINK YOU'RE RIGHT TO HIDE OUT HERE TILL YOU DECIDE WHAT TO DO NEXT!
IT'S ALL SO CONFUSING.

BUT I FEEL NOW THAT I CAN SPEAK TO HUMANS, THERE ARE SO MANY THINGS I'D LIKE TO SAY,......

I THINK YOU SHOULD JUST BE A SPOKESMAN FOR THE ANIMAL KINGDOM! YOU'D REALLY HAVE **CREDIBILITY!**
REALLY? WHY?

1·11
WELL, FOR ONE THING, YOU'VE NEVER WORN **FUR!**
I GUESS THAT'S TRUE!

SO THAT'S THE STORY. THIS DOLPHIN AT THE HEALTH CLUB LEARNED ENGLISH IN THE U.S. NAVY!

I PROMISED TO KEEP HIS SECRET! WHEN HE DECIDES WHAT HE WANTS TO DO, I'M GOING TO HELP!
1·12

WELL, WE WON'T TELL ANYONE! JUST LET US KNOW WHEN HE DECIDES WHAT HE WANTS TO DO!

I THINK CRANBROOK IS ABOUT TO CROSS FROM THE MERELY ECCENTRIC INTO THE **TRULY STRANGE!**
SINCLAIR

WHY CAN'T YOU JUST ADMIT YOU TALKED TO A DOLPHIN AND HE TALKED BACK?
NOPE. I PUT IT OUT OF MY MIND. JUST LEAVE ME OUT OF IT.
HOW CAN YOU SAY THAT?
EASY. AND IF YOU SEE ANY FLYING SAUCERS, LEAVE ME OUT OF THAT, TOO. I DON'T GET INVOLVED IN WEIRDNESS.
HE SAYS YOU'RE PRETTY COOL, FOR A HUMAN!
PRETTY FAINT PRAISE, THAT.
HE ALSO THINKS YOU HAVE A HIGH VIBRATION.
THAT'S JUST WHAT I'M TALKIN' ABOUT!
1·14

I DON'T THINK A TALKING DOLPHIN CAN STAY SECRET FOR VERY LONG.

EVEN ROIDZ IS STARTING TO SUSPECT SOMETHING.
1·15

OK! WHO'S THE WISE GUY?
PREMISES GUARDED BY ATTACK DOLPHIN.
NO, I'M NOT A FISH— I'M A MAMMAL
YES, I BITE
YES, YOU CAN FEED ME. WATCH YOUR FINGERS

WHAT IF SOMEONE UNSCRUPULOUS FINDS OUT OUT ABOUT "FLIPPY"?
1·16

SOMEONE WHO DOESN'T CAR ABOUT HIM, OR HIS WELFARE, OR HIS GOALS.

BUT WHO WOULD THINK LIKE THAT?

I'M JUST WORRIED THAT SOMEONE IS GOING TO TRY TO TAKE ADVANTAGE OF "FLIPPY".
SINCLAIR

THAT'S CRAZY. WHAT DO PEOPLE HAVE THAT A DOLPHIN COULD WANT? MONEY? GIVE ME A BREAK!

1·17
WHAT'S "MUNNY"?

I KNOW YOU WANT TO COMMUNICATE WITH PEOPLE, BUT YOU'LL NEED MONEY! NOBODY WILL LISTEN TO YOU IF YOU DON'T HAVE MONEY!

TO GET MONEY, YOU NEED AN AGENT! I CAN BE YOUR AGENT!
WHAT'S AN AGENT?
1·18
SINCLAIR

SOMEONE WHO KEEPS YOUR MONEY!
WOW! YOU'D DO THAT FOR ME?

OF COURSE! I'LL KEEP IT ALL IN A BANK FOR YOU!
GREAT! WHAT'S A BANK?

HEY, CRANBROOK! LOOK! I'VE GOT SOME NEW FRIENDS WHO WILL HELP ME GET MONEY!
SINCLAIR

REMORA IS TELLING ME ALL I NEED TO KNOW!
I'D BE CAREFUL, FLIPPY...

HOW WILL THEY MAKE MONEY FOR YOU?

TELL ME AGAIN,.. WHO WAS THIS..... MISTER ED?
HOW CAN YOU LIVE WITH YOURSELF?
1·19

FLIPPY, DON'T LISTEN TO THESE PEOPLE. THEY'RE HERE TO TAKE ADVANTAGE OF YOU! YOU DON'T NEED THEIR MONEY!

BUT HOW WILL I GET BY? I'M A STRANGER IN A STRANGE LAND!
BUT YOU HAVE SOME UNIQUE ABILITIES!
WITH YOUR SWIMMING AND DIVING SKILLS, I'M SURE YOU COULD DO SOMETHING EXCITING AND CREATIVE,...

...LIKE FIGHTING OIL SPILLS. OR SNIFFING OUT **SEWAGE** AND **TOXIC WASTE**!
RIGHT! EASY FOR **YOU** TO SAY!
1-21

HEY, BUTT OUT! FLIPPY, HERE, CAN MAKE UP HIS OWN MIND ABOUT WHAT HE WANTS IN HIS NEW LIFE! WE'RE JUST HELPING HIM DECIDE!

WE'RE TRYING TO ACQUAINT HIM WITH THE **BEST** THAT OUR COUNTRY HAS TO OFFER!
YEAH!
GAME SHOWS! DREAM VACATIONS! FABULOUS PRIZES! CARNIVAL CRUISES!
WOW!
SPORTY COUPES! THE LUXURY OF RICH CORINTHIAN LEATHER!
WHAT'S THAT?! WHAT'S THAT?!!
1-22
I'D LIKE TO JUST GO BACK TO THE OCEAN-- BUT YOU HAVE TO UNDERSTAND,.... THE GREATEST **EXTINCTION** IN 60 MILLION YEARS IS GOING ON RIGHT NOW!

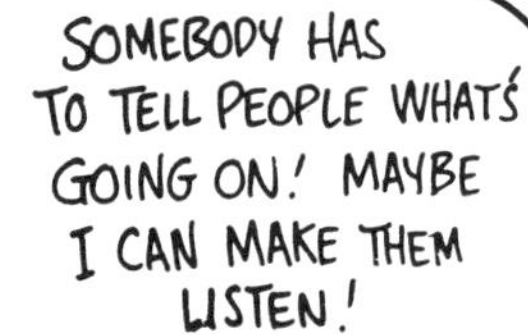

SOMEBODY HAS TO TELL PEOPLE WHAT'S GOING ON! MAYBE I CAN MAKE THEM LISTEN!

1-23
YOU MEAN, SO THEY'LL SAVE THE **PLANET**?

HEY, THE **PLANET'S** GONNA BE HERE! BUT IF I WAS YOU, I'D BE THINKIN' ABOUT SAVIN' MY **BUTT**!

LOOK, EVERYBODY SAYS "SAVE THE WHALES," BUT IT'S NOT JUST THE WHALES THAT ARE IN TROUBLE!

IT'S THE ENTIRE OCEAN WITH EVERY CREATURE IN IT THAT'S THREATENED.
1·24

AND THAT'S CONNECTED TO EVERY LAND CREATURE, TO THE AIR YOU BREATHE, YOUR WEATHER,... EVERYTHING!

YOU MEAN, IT SHOULD BE LIKE,... "SAVE THE WHOLES"?
EXACTLY!

MAYBE PEOPLE WOULD LISTEN TO ME SINCE I'M NOT HUMAN! I'D TELL THEM THE TRUTH!
BE CAREFUL.
1·25
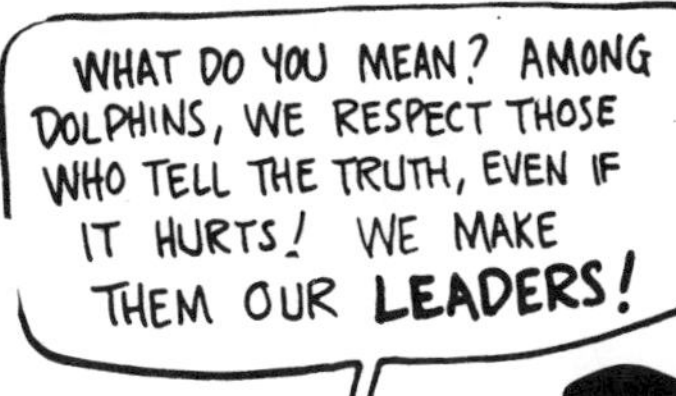
WHAT DO YOU MEAN? AMONG DOLPHINS, WE RESPECT THOSE WHO TELL THE TRUTH, EVEN IF IT HURTS! WE MAKE THEM OUR LEADERS!

SINCLAIR

WELL, IT'S CONSIDERABLY DIFFERENT AMONG HUMANS.
HOW SO?
DOES THE NAME "GEORGE BUSH" MEAN ANYTHING TO YOU?
NO. SHOULD IT?

UH-OH,.... HERE COMES ROIDZ, HE DOESN'T KNOW ABOUT YOU YET!
WELL, IT'S TIME HE FOUND OUT!

DON'T SEND ME BACK! I'LL DO ANYTHING! I'LL GIVE RIDES TO ALL THE CRANKY KIDS AND WEIRD OLD LADIES! JUST LET ME HIDE OUT HERE FOR A WHILE!
?
SINCLAIR
OH,.. SURE!..... STICK AROUND! I'LL PUT YOU ON STAFF AND GIVE YOU A SALARY!
GREAT!
!!?
1·26
YEAH. NOW JUST LET ME TALK TO MY LITTLE BUDDY HERE.......
?
PRETTY GOOD, EH? I DIDN'T EVEN BLINK! NOW, WHAT'S REALLY GOING ON HERE?

WELL, YOUR NEWEST EMPLOYEE IS, UM,... BODACIOUS,.... LOQUACIOUS,... AND CETACEOUS!

I WAS WATCHIN' THAT SHOW, "911 HOMICIDE." IT'S WHATCHA CALL "REALITY T.V.",...... REAL LIFE STUFF!
OH, I STOPPED WATCHING IT.

YOU, KNOW, PEOPLE DON'T SEEM TO REALIZE THEY'RE NOT SHARING A REAL EXPERIENCE.

PEOPLE FORGET THAT, IN REALITY, WHAT THEY'RE DOING IS SITTING IN A DARK ROOM, WATCHING A GLOWING, PHOSPHORESCENT TUBE!

THAT'S WHY I'VE SWITCHED TO JUST WATCHING BLANK CHANNELS OR TEST PATTERNS.

IT'S A PURER EXPERIENCE.
SURE,... I CAN SEE THAT,.....

THIS IS MY "INTUITION TRAINING EXERCISE." LIKE MANY SUCCESSFUL PEOPLE, I'M TRAINING MY HIDDEN INTUITIVE POWERS.

AS I RELAX, I GET MORE IN TOUCH WITH MY SUBCONSCIOUS MIND. AT THIS POINT, I AM TOTALLY RECEPTIVE.
2·11

YOU MAY ASK ME... **ANYTHING.**

WHEN ARE YOU GOING TO CLEAN THE MEN'S ROOM?
IT'S HAZY..... VERY HAZY.......

MANY GREAT MEN USED PERIODS OF RELAXATION TO DEVELOP THEIR MINDS. IT'S SAID THAT DESCARTES FORMULATED HIS THEORY OF ANALYTIC GEOMETRY.....

.....WHILE LYING IN BED WATCHING A FLY CRAWL ON THE CEILING.

2·12

IF I RELAX HERE LONG ENOUGH, I'M SURE A VALUABLE REALIZATION WILL HIT ME IN THE FACE.

YOU'RE RIGHT. I THINK IT WON'T BE LONG.
YOU THINK SO?

I DON'T KNOW WHAT'S WRONG WITH ME. I NEVER HAVE ANY MONEY! I GUESS I'LL ALWAYS JUST BE POOR!

DON'T THINK OF IT SO NEGATIVELY. PERHAPS YOU CAN BE HELPED.

YOU MAY NOT BE "POOR," BUT SIMPLY A "FISCAL UNDERACHIEVER." YOU MAY BE SUFFERING FROM A COMMON "**EARNING DISORDER**".
2·13
YOU MAY BE JUST ONE OF THE MILLIONS WHO ARE "**MOOLAH IMPAIRED**"!
YOU MEAN THERE'S **HOPE**?
OF COURSE!

CHAD, YOU'RE AN AD-MAN, HELP ME COME UP WITH A SNAPPY NEW SLOGAN FOR THE CAFE,... SOMETHING THAT EXPRESSES OUR PHILOSOPHY.....
WHICH IS......?
SINCLAIR

WE WANT PEOPLE TO FEEL THAT OUR SIMPLE, HEALTHY, LOW-FAT CUISINE CAN HELP THEM REACH THEIR TRUE POTENTIAL!

HOW 'BOUT EAT,... ALL THAT YOU CAN EAT!
GREAT!
2·14

LOOK! I GOT MY NEW SUBLIMINAL SELF-IMPROVEMENT VIDEO!

THIS ONE'S CALLED "OVERCOMING FEARS AND PHOBIAS."
OH YEAH. I KNEW A GUY THAT USED THAT ONE FOR HIS FEAR OF HEIGHTS!
SINCLAIR

DID IT WORK?
OH YEAH!

WITHIN TWO WEEKS HE WENT AND JUMPED OFF A BRIDGE!
2·15

SPECIAL
NUT-OAT-BRAN
WHEATBERRY
RADISH SOUP
I'LL NEVER UNDERSTAND WHY YOU MAKE FOOD THIS WAY. IT'S LIKE,... SO PRIMITIVE!

WE TRY TO GO BACK TO THE FOODS OUR ANCESTORS ATE TRADITIONALLY.

YOU KNOW,... THE FOODS OUR SPECIES EVOLVED ON WAY BACK THRU TIME.
?

YOU MEAN LIKE SPAM? CHEERIOS?
FURTHER BACK.....
2·16
SINCLAIR

ACCORDING TO THIS BOOK, I MAY BE WHAT THEY CALL A "CO-DEPENDENT PERSONALITY"!
WHAT'S THAT MEAN?

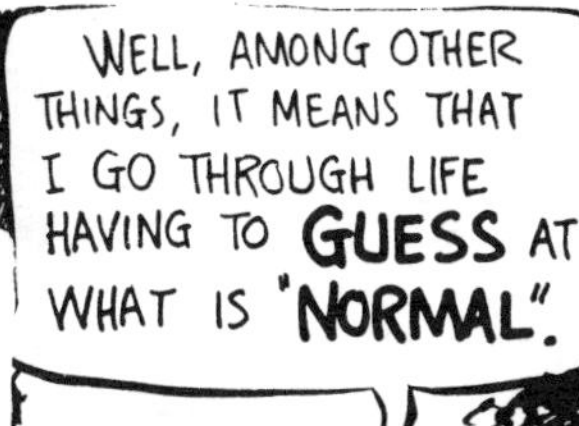
WELL, AMONG OTHER THINGS, IT MEANS THAT I GO THROUGH LIFE HAVING TO GUESS AT WHAT IS "NORMAL".

2·18

GUESS AGAIN.

FEW PEOPLE REALIZE THAT WITHIN EACH OF US IS AN "INNER CHILD."

THE INNER CHILD MUST BE NURTURED AND CARED FOR!
2·19
FROM NOW ON, I'M GOING TO SIT DOWN AND CHAT WITH MY INNER CHILD EVERY DAY!

WELL, THERE HE GOES,..... THE INNER CHILD FROM OUTER SPACE!

YOU'RE LATE AGAIN!

YES, BUT REMEMBER,.... EINSTEIN SHOWED THAT WE LIVE IN A NON-SIMULTANEOUS UNIVERSE!
IN FACT, IF THIS CAFE WAS MOVING AT THE SPEED OF LIGHT,... I'D BE AT LEAST TEN MINUTES EARLY!
WELL, WARP YOUR BUTT INTO THE KITCHEN AND DO THOSE DISHES!
DON'T WORRY! SPEAKING FOURTH DIMENSIONALLY, THEY'RE ALREADY DONE!
2·20

YOU PEOPLE THINK YOU'RE SO SMART WITH ALL THIS TRENDY FOOD! BUT I WAS READIN' HOW DIETICIANS SAY GOOD OLD AMERICAN FOOD IS JUST **FINE**!

YOU'RE NOT DIETICIANS! WHAT DO YOU KNOW ?! I BET NOT ONE OF YOU IS A **DIETICIAN**!

DIETICIAN?

2·21
YOU KNOW,... THE PEOPLE WHO MAKE THE DELICIOUS MEALS IN **SCHOOLS** AND **HOSPITALS**!
SURE! GO AHEAD AND MAKE FUN!

YOU KNOW, I THINK POLLUTION IS NATURE'S WAY OF TELLING US WE'RE ON THE WRONG ROAD.
AHH,... I THINK IT'S EXAGGERATED.

REALLY, THOUGH,... ...I THINK THE UNIVERSE SPEAKS TO US IN MANY MYSTERIOUS WAYS!
ARE YOU SERIOUS?

YES! I DEFINITELY THINK THE UNIVERSE IS TELLING US SOMETHING!

WELL, THE **UNIVERSE** IS **WRONG**!
YOU THINK SO?
HECK YEAH! IT WOULDN'T BE THE **FIRST** TIME, FER GOSH SAKES!
2·22

HEY, LOOK! HERE'S MY LATEST **SUBLIMINAL SELF-IMPROVEMENT** VIDEO!

IT'S CALLED, "REMOVING BLOCKS TO YOUR SUCCESS".
OH YEAH. I KNOW A GUY WHO USED THAT ONE!

2·23
REALLY? DID IT WORK?
YOU BET!

HE SHOT HIS BOSS!

ONE PERCENT INSPIRATION, NINETY-NINE PERCENT PERSPIRATION!
2·25

YOU MEAN THE "FORMULA FOR CREATIVITY"?

NOPE. IT'S WHAT THIS COFFEE TASTES LIKE!

I'M SO FED UP WITH MY JOB! IT'S LIKE, MY BOSS THINKS HE OWNS ME!

WELL, THIS IS ONE GUY THAT CAN'T BE BOUGHT!
SINCLAIR

BUT HAVEN'T YOU BEEN DOING THAT JOB FOR FIFTEEN YEARS NOW?
2·26

LEASED! NOT BOUGHT!

I'M JUST AT A DEAD END. THERE'S NO SATISFACTION IN MY WORK. I DON'T KNOW HOW I GOT INTO IT!

YOU KNOW, THEY SAY TO BE HAPPY YOU MUST "FOLLOW YOUR BLISS"!
2·27
SINCLAIR

NO WONDER!

I'VE BEEN FOLLOWING MY BLISTERS.

I JUST CAN'T SEEM TO SNAP OUT OF THIS!
THAT BAD, EH?

YEAH, IVE BEEN DOWN LIKE THIS FOR A WEEK!
2·28
SINCLAIR

I GUESS I JUST FEEL COMPLETELY DISILLUSIONED.

SO IS THIS A SIMPLE BLUE FUNK, TRUE CLINICAL DEPRESSION, MID-LIFE CRISIS OR FULL-BLOWN "BIG CHILL"?
I JUST LIKED IT BETTER BEING "ILLUSIONED"

HEY, CRANBROOK! SUIT UP! I'VE GOT A DEPRESSED CLIENT WHO NEEDS SOME OF YOUR "CLOWNSELING"!
NOW DON'T MAKE A BIG DEAL ABOUT IT!

CRANBROOK IS A TIME-HUMOR THERAPIST! I THINK YOU COULD USE SOME!
YOU KNOW WHAT THEY SAY, "A MERRY HEART DOETH GOOD LIKE A MEDICINE"!

"HUMOR THERAPY"? "CLOWNSELING"? YOU GOTTA BE JOKING!

DON'T MAKE ME LAUGH.
ARE YOU SURE YOU'RE CLEAR ON THE CONCEPT HERE?
3·1

HERE I AM TRYING TO BE MISERABLE...AND YOU'RE MAKING JOKES!

WHERE DO YOU GET OFF WITH THAT ATTITUDE?

BUT HUMOR IS THE BEST RESPONSE TO MOST THINGS IN LIFE!
3·2
SINCLAIR

THE UNIVERSE IS, AFTER ALL, A JOKE THAT NOBODY QUITE GETS!

HEY, C'MON OVER HERE! THERE'S SOMETHING I WANT TO SHOW YOU!

HERE. TRY THIS ON.
A WORKOUT SUIT?

NOT REALLY. THIS IS A PRODUCT OF THE LATEST SOVIET RESEARCH!
3·4
SINCLAIR

IT'S KIND OF BAGGY....
WELL, THE RUSSIANS DON'T HAVE A REAL FEEL FOR SPANDEX YET.

CRANBROOK IS TRYING ON THE LATEST IN SOVIET WORKOUT SUITS,....
IT'S A LITTLE LARGE,.. BUT WE CAN TAKE IT IN.....

ONCE YOU START WEARING IT, YOU'LL MAKE FASTER PROGRESS. IT USES SPECIAL ELECTRONIC IMPULSES...
3·5

TO DIRECTLY STIMULATE ALL YOUR MAJOR MUSCLE GROUPS!
WOW! I FEEL STRONGER ALREADY!
SINCLAIR

I NEVER THOUGHT OF MYSELF AS HAVING MAJOR MUSCLE GROUPS!

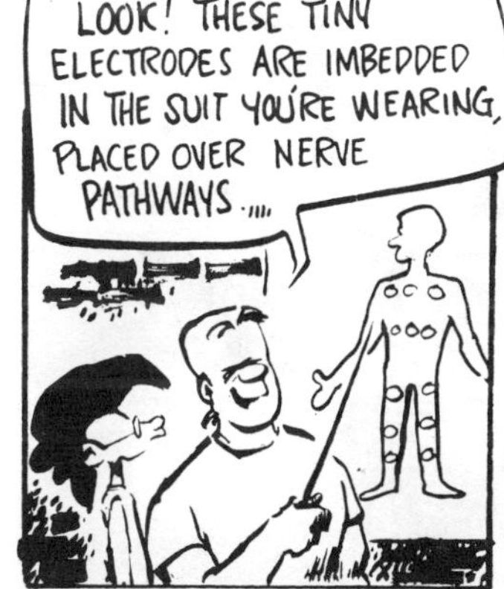
LOOK! THESE TINY ELECTRODES ARE IMBEDDED IN THE SUIT YOU'RE WEARING, PLACED OVER NERVE PATHWAYS.....

CONTROLLED IN SEQUENCE BY A TINY COMPUTER!
3·6

SO THAT EVEN AS YOU WORK, IT WILL STIMULATE YOUR MUSCLES IN SLOW, RHYTHMIC CONTRACTIONS!
SLOW, RHYTHMIC CONTRACTIONS! GREAT! THAT'S HOW I LIKE TO WORK ANYWAY!

ALEX! IS CRANBROOK WORKING? LOOK, HE'S WEARING A SPECIAL SUIT AND THERE'S SOMETHING HE SHOULD KNOW!
I WAS JUST READING THE INSTRUCTIONS AND HE SHOULD KNOW HE'S GOT TO WATCH OUT FOR **OUTSIDE ELECTRICAL SOURCES**!

THE CIRCUITS IN HIS SUIT MIGHT BE CAPTURED BY AN OUTSIDE SIGNAL, LIKE MAYBE A **CARDIAC PACEMAKER**!
SINCLAIR
3·7

MEANWHILE
YOUNG MAN, I'D LIKE TO SAMPLE THE "CORONARY CLEAN-OUT SPECIAL."
PING PING PING PING

THE DELICATE ELECTRONICS OF CRANBROOK'S CYBERNETIC BIO-ELECTRONIC-STIMULATION UNDER-GARMENT HAVE BEEN CAPTURED BY SIGNALS FROM A CUSTOMER'S CARDIAC PACEMAKER!

SPROING

ZIP!

CRANBROOK, ARE **YOU** O.K.?
COULD YOU OPEN THE DOOR, PLEASE.
3·8

AAALIGH!
LOOK OUT!
SINCLAIR

THANK YOU.
3·9

IT'S O.K., FOLKS, JUST PART OF OUR COMMITMENT TO **HIRE** THE **STRANGE**!
I'M CALLING FOR HELP!
SPROING!

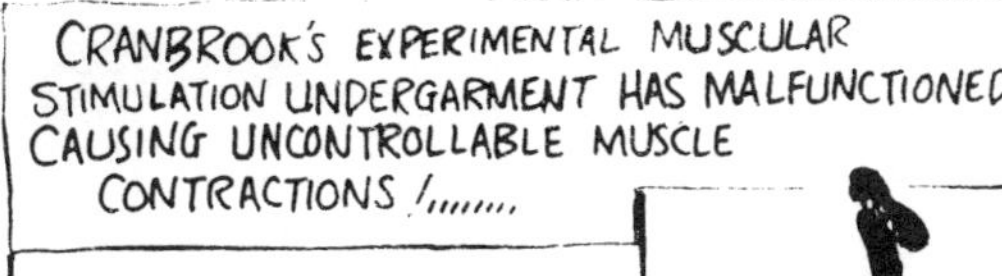
CRANBROOK'S EXPERIMENTAL MUSCULAR STIMULATION UNDERGARMENT HAS MALFUNCTIONED, CAUSING UNCONTROLLABLE MUSCLE CONTRACTIONS!.......

SHOOM!
3·11

WONG!

FOOP!
SINCLAIR

ALPHA 105...... MILL ROAD NEAR CHERRY ST..... IT'S EITHER A PSYCHOTIC BREAK, OR A BREAK-DANCING PSYCHOTIC.....
GREAT. JUST GREAT.

IT'S TOTALLY UNLIKE CRANBROOK! HE JUST BOLTED INTO THE STREET AND STARTED BOUNCING AROUND!

THEN HE DISAPPEARRED. WE CAN'T FIND HIM ANYWHERE!

LOOK, I'M SURE YOUR FRIEND HAS GONE HOME TO SLEEP IT OFF BY NOW.
SINCLAIR

WAIT! THERE HE IS!
RATS.
3·12

THEY ALWAYS COME OUT ON MY SHIFT.....

OOOF! HE'S AS STRONG AS A BULL! MUST BE ON PCP!
SINCLAIR

LOOK OUT!
ROARRR
3·13

ROARR

IT STOPPED. WE MUST BE OUT OF RANGE.
WHAT STOPPED?

INVISIBLE RAYS WERE CONTROLLING THE MUSCLES IN MY BODY.
OH,... YEAH.
3·14
SINCLAIR

I CAN'T THANK YOU ENOUGH FOR........
WE NEED TO TALK....

I REALIZE THIS IS RATHER UNUSUAL, BUT I HOPE YOU WON'T THINK THIS IS TYPICAL OF HOW WE OPERATE HERE.....
3·15

LOOK, BUD, I'M SURE YOUR RESTAURANT IS A FINE EATING ESTABLISHMENT, AND YOUR HIRING PRACTICES ARE YOUR BUSINESS, BUT BETWEEN YOU AND ME......
SINCLAIR

I THINK YOU SHOULD TAKE A SERIOUS LOOK AT WHERE YOUR MUSHROOMS ARE COMING FROM.
I STOPPED TWITCHING. CAN I GET UP NOW?

PRRING
GOOD MORNING, THIS IS ALEX'S RESTAURANT.

THAT'S RIGHT, MA'AM, WE SERVE MOSTLY HEALTHY-TYPE STUFF,... GRAINS, GREENS TOFU,......
TOFU....
TO-FU. IT'S A GOOD SOURCE OF PROTEIN.
SINCLAIR

?

NO, MA'AM, YOU'RE THINKING OF TOE JAM.
3·16

I SENT CRANBROOK OUT TO BUY AN AQUARIUM!

I THOUGHT IT WOULD BE A GREAT STRESS REDUCER FOR OUR CUSTOMERS!

I READ THAT JUST SITTING WITH AN AQUARIUM CAN PRODUCE A RELAXED, ALMOST MEDITATIVE STATE!
I'M BACK!

THEY WERE ALL OUT OF AQUARIUMS.

BUT DON'T WORRY,... I GOT THE NEXT BEST THING!
?

O.K., TELL ME AGAIN. WHAT'S SO RELAXING ABOUT AN ANT FARM?

HERE I AM, HENNA PENNYROYAL, READY TO BEGIN A NEW CHAPTER IN MY LIFE! A FREE, STRONG AND INDEPENDENT WOMAN AT LAST!

GREAT TO SEE YOU! YOU'LL BE WORKING THE HOURS WE TALKED ABOUT.....
GREAT!
SINCLAIR

I WANT YOU TO MEET CRANBROOK WILSON. HE'LL BE SORT OF SUPERVISING YOU AND SHOWING YOU THE ROPES. I THINK YOU'LL SEE HE'S PRETTY LAID-BACK!

CRANBROOK, THIS IS.....
GET TO WORK.....
3·18

SO, THE NEW WAITRESS IS HERE?
YUP! CRANBROOK IS TRAINING HER NOW!
SINCLAIR

TRAINING HER?
WELL, HE SAID HE WAS GOING TO USE SPECIAL ROLE-PLAYING EXERCISES TO PREPARE HER FOR ANY EMERGENCY!

O.K., HERE'S THE SITUATION. YOU'RE COMMANDER OF A STARSHIP LOST IN THE NEGATIVE ZONE. YOUR DILITHIUM CRYSTALS ARE EXHAUSTED.......
3·19

O.K. HERE'S A LIST OF YOUR DUTIES. SWEEPING, MOPPING, DISHWASHING, BUSSING TABLES, SALAD PREP, WAITING TABLES,....

MAINTAINING COUNTERTOPS, REPLENISHING CONDIMENTS, WATERING PLANTS, CLEANING REFRIGERATOR...

CLEANING STOVE, WASHING WINDOWS, SWEEPING SIDEWALK, TAKE OUT GARBAGE, HANDLE RECYCLABLES...
SINCLAIR

WHAT WILL YOU BE DOING?
PRIMARILY, PLANNING AND ESTABLISHING A THEORETICAL FRAMEWORK FOR...
HEY,.. CRANBROOK GET THE POOPER SCOOPER AND HIT THE FRONT SIDEWALK!
3·20

HI. I'M HENNA. AS PART OF OUR CONCEPT OF TOTAL SERVICE, I'LL BE GIVING YOU A RELAXING FOOT MASSAGE WHILE YOU WAIT FOR YOUR MEAL!

?

WELL, GEE, THAT SOUNDS NICE.....

AAHH....
OOPS...
HEY....
WHOA.....

STOP! YOU'RE KILLING ME!
TRY TO RELAX. YOU GOT QUITE A BIT OF TENSION HERE....

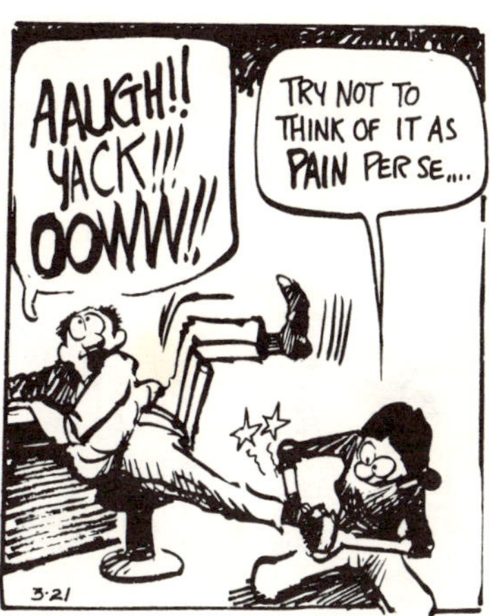
AAUGH!! YACK!!! OOWW!!
TRY NOT TO THINK OF IT AS PAIN PER SE....
3·21

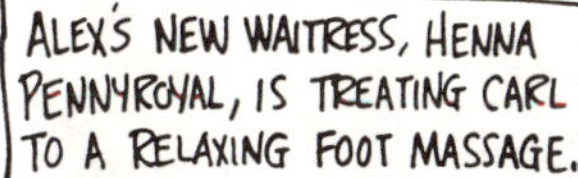
ALEX'S NEW WAITRESS, HENNA PENNYROYAL, IS TREATING CARL TO A RELAXING FOOT MASSAGE...

AAAUGH!
RELAX NOW, BREATHE THROUGH IT....

AUGH! ACH! EEECK!
UH.... EVERYTHING O.K. HERE?
OH YES!

EEEPH....
I THINK HE'S RELIVING HIS BIRTH TRAUMA!

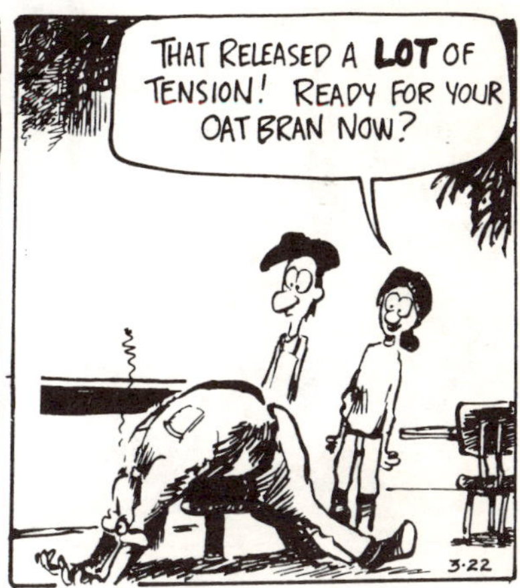
THAT RELEASED A LOT OF TENSION! READY FOR YOUR OAT BRAN NOW?
3·22

WHOA! WHAT DID YOU DO? THAT REALLY HURT!
BUT IT WAS "GOOD PAIN," WASN'T IT?
3·23

WHAT ARE YOU? SOME KINDA SADIST? YOU WERE PULLIN' MY TOES OUT!

I THINK I'VE TAPPED INTO THE REPRESSED EMOTIONS THAT YOU'VE NEVER SHARED.... ALL STORED IN YOUR FEET!
WHAT?

NUMBER ONE - I DON'T HAVE ANY REPRESSED EMOTIONS. NUMBER TWO, I COULDN'T CARE LESS, AND NUMBER THREE, IT'S NONE OF YOUR BEESWAX!
HMM... I THINK I'D BETTER SCHEDULE YOU 3 TIMES A WEEK...

LET'S SEE HOW OL' FLIPPY'S DOING.....
POOL

HEY! LITTLE EAGLE! MY FAVORITE MEDICINE MAN! YOU AND FLIPPY KNOW EACH OTHER?
YUP!

SURE! I'M TEACHING HIM THE NATIVE AMERICAN MEDICINE WAY!

3·25
YEAH! AND I'M TEACHING HIM ALL ABOUT UNDERWATER DEMOLITION AND COMBAT TECHNIQUES!

SO, HOW DID YOU FIRST BECOME A MEDICINE MAN?
WELL, I STARTED OUT AS A TRUCKDRIVER, BUT THEN, I STARTED LEARNING MORE ABOUT MY ROOTS......

MY GRANDFATHER SENT ME OUT IN THE WOODS FOR FOUR DAYS WITH NO FOOD OR WATER!
WOW! WHAT HAPPENED?

WELL, I HAD A DREAM WHERE THE GREAT SPIRIT TOLD ME TO STUDY THE HEALING WAY!

SO YOU STOPPED TRUCKDRIVING AND BECAME A FULL-TIME MEDICINE MAN?
OH, NO,.. THE GREAT SPIRIT ALSO TOLD ME NOT TO GIVE UP MY DAY JOB!
THE OL' GREAT SPIRIT KNOWS THE SCORE, I GUESS....
3·26

SO LITTLE EAGLE, HERE, HAS BEEN DOING HIS SWEAT LODGE CEREMONY RIGHT HERE AT THE HEALTH CLUB! IT'S THE FIRST THING WARRIORS LEARN!
WOW!

I WANNA DO IT! DO YOU THINK I CAN BE AN INDIAN WARRIOR?

WELL, MAYBE. BUT THERE IS MUCH TO LEARN. THE SWEAT LODGE IS CRUCIAL, BUT IT'S ONLY THE BEGINNING.
LET'S GET STARTED! I WANT TO DO IT ALL!

FIRST OF ALL.... WHAT'S SWEAT?
O.K., LET'S START WITH SOME FUNDAMENTALS....
3·27

THE NEXT THING A WARRIOR MUST DO IS OBSERVE THE ANIMAL KINGDOM. HE MUST STUDY THE SPECIAL GIFTS OF EACH CREATURE.

THE GRACE OF THE DEER, THE POWER OF THE LION,.. THE SPEED OF THE HAWK,...
PEOPLE TODAY RARELY SEE THESE ANIMALS, OR APPRECIATE THEIR SPECIAL VIRTUES.
STILL, THOUGH, I CAN PONDER THE PATIENCE OF MY GOLDFISH, THE STEALTH OF THE COCKROACH,...
.... THE FLEXIBILITY OF MY WACKY WALLWALKER,...

OF COURSE, THE REASON YOUR PEOPLE HAVE NO CONNECTION TO NATURE IS YOU'RE TOO BUSY DESTROYING IT!

YOU KNOW, WE COULD LOSE MORE SPECIES IN THE NEXT 20 YEARS THAN WE HAVE IN THE LAST 20 MILLION!

I KNOW, I KNOW,.... I AGREE WITH YOU! BUT.....

....IN DEFENSE OF MY CIVILIZATION, MAY I JUST SAY WE'VE MADE SOME REAL BREAKTHROUGHS IN CONVENIENCE PACKAGING AND MICROWAVABLE TV DINNERS.

THESE NUMBERS DON'T LOOK GOOD.....

WE COULD LOSE OUR SHIRTS IF WE DON'T LOOK OUT!

RELAX! SOME PEOPLE MAKE A MILLION, LOSE A MILLION, MAKE A MILLION AND LOSE IT AGAIN!
YEAH,.. BUT I'D KNOW WHEN TO STOP!

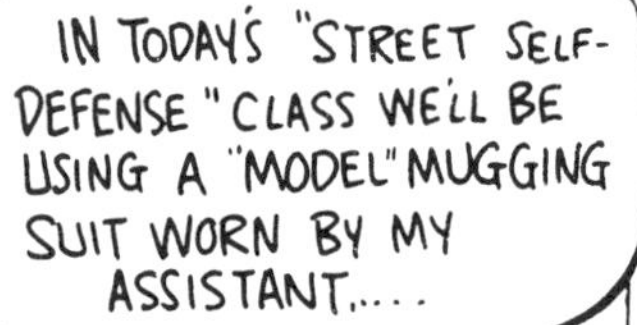
IN TODAY'S "STREET SELF-DEFENSE" CLASS WE'LL BE USING A "MODEL" MUGGING SUIT WORN BY MY ASSISTANT.....

IN THIS PROTECTIVE GEAR,... HE WILL BE SIMULATING AN ATTACK, WHICH YOU WILL LEARN TO DEFEND AGAINST...

..YOU CAN VISUALIZE YOURSELF WALKING ON A LONELY STREET, WHEN SUDDENLY...... UNEXPECTEDLY.......
4-1
SINCLAIR

... I GET MUGGED BY A GUMBY?
NATURALLY WE HAVE TO USE OUR IMAGINATIONS....

YOU MAY DEFEND YOURSELF IN ANY WAY YOU LIKE. YOU CAN'T HURT THE SIMULATED "MUGGER"
WOP WOP
WOP WOP

BE AGGRESSIVE! REMEMBER, IN THIS SITUATION ANYTHING GOES! BITING, SCRATCHING, EYE GOUGING....
WHUP?
4-2

...HAIR PULLING....
AAAUGH!!
UNHH!...
RRIP!
SINCLAIR

GEE, ARE YOU OK?
IT'S ALL RIGHT, MA'AM. HE'S BEEN PREPARED FOR THIS!

WELL, THIS IS ALL VERY WELL FOR THE UNARMED MUGGER.... BUT WHAT IF HE WAS ARMED..?

WHAT IF HE'S GOT A WAZOO?
4-3

YOU KNOW, THOSE WAZOOS THEY HAVE... LIKE ON "MIAMI VICE."

YOU MEAN AN "UZI"?
YEAH, RIGHT,.... ONE OF THOSE.

WHAT I WANT YOU TO REMEMBER ABOUT SELF-DEFENSE IS THIS.....

4-4

YOU MUST STRIP THE ATTACKER'S DEFENSE...
RRIP

... EXPOSE HIS WEAKNESSES.....
?
TWHIP
SINCLAIR

...AND ATTACK SENSITIVE, VITAL POINTS!
AAUGH!! NO "NOOGIES"! PLEASE! NO "NOOGIES"!!

OFTEN, A WELL-PREPARED CITIZEN MAY DECIDE TO CARRY SMALL BUT EFFECTIVE SELF-DEFENSE WEAPONS.
4-5

FOR INSTANCE, UPON BEING ATTACKED, THIS CITIZEN REACHES FOR HIS RAZOR-SHARP, NINJA THROWING STARS!

...AND HURLS THEM WITH LETHAL FORCE!..... AND... UH.... HURLS THEM......
URK...

...AND HURLS THEM WITH LETHAL FORCE...... WHAT IS IT?
DO YOU HAVE ANY BAND-AIDS?

FINALLY, WE LOOK AT THE ABILITY TO IMPROVISE IN A SELF-DEFENSE TACTIC EVEN IN THE HOME. JOANNE HERE WILL SIMULATE A HOMEMAKER....
4-6

....ATTACKED UNEXPECTEDLY IN HER KITCHEN..... THINKING QUICKLY, SHE WHEELS AROUND.....
SINCLAIR

SPORK!
....IN THIS CASE, BLASTING THE INTRUDER WITH A SALAD SHOOTER!
ARE YOU OK?
FINE. GOT ANY DRESSING?

HEY, ALEX, I GOT THAT ORDER OF YOURS...
GREAT!

SAY, CARL, HAVE YOU MET RUSTY HATCHWAY? HE GROWS SOME OUR ORGANIC VEGGIES!
HOWDY!
OH,.. HI,...
SINCLAIR

NOW YOUR NAME IS FAMILIAR,.... HMMM, RUSTY HATCHWAY,... SAY,... YOU WOULDN'T BE....

.. THE ASTRONAUT!?
YUP. WHERE DO YA WANT THESE SPUDS, ALEX?
4.15

CARL MEETS ASTRONAUT-TURNED-FARMER RUSTY HATCHWAY.....
WELL, IT'S LIKE I NEEDED TO GET AWAY FROM THE PLANET TO REALLY SEE IT CLEARLY.....

I MEAN, THERE WAS THE SUN, AND THE PLANETS, AND THE STARS, AND THE EARTH,... AND ME! AND SOMEHOW, I FELT LIKE I WAS PART OF IT ALL,...

AND, IT WAS LIKE, I WAS SUPPOSED TO BE THERE. AND, IT WAS ALL ALIVE,... ...SOMEHOW,... AND EVEN FRIENDLY SOMEHOW....
4.16

SO YOU THINK THE TAXPAYERS SENT YOU TO THE MOON JUST SO YOU COULD SPACE OUT LIKE THAT?
I DON'T KNOW. I JUST DONT KNOW......

SO DO OTHER ASTRONAUTS HAVE THE SAME GOOFY IDEAS YOU DO?
YES.

IN FACT, I BELONG TO THE ASSOCIATION OF SPACE EXPLORERS, AND WE'VE BEEN WORKING ON A LOT OF IDEAS...
4.17

LIKE, IF WE COULD JUST SEND ALL THE WORLD'S POLITICIANS TO THE MOON.....
WHOA! STOP RIGHT THERE!

THAT'S THE ANSWER! IT'S SO OBVIOUS! COULD WE SEND THE LAWYERS, TOO?
WAIT, I'M NOT FINISHED..

HEY, ALEX! C'MERE! MY MAN RUSTY HERE HAS THE IDEA OF THE CENTURY! AND I THOUGHT THE SPACE PROGRAM WAS IMPRACTICAL ALL THIS TIME.....
SINCLAIR

RUSTY WAS JUST TELLIN' ME ABOUT HOW WE SHOULD SEND ALL THE WORLD'S POLITICIANS TO THE MOON! IS THAT BEAUTIFUL?.....

I MEAN, IT'S SIMPLICITY ITSELF! IT'S FOOLPROOF! IT'S SHEER GENIUS!
YES. THEY COULD ALL SEE THE EARTH AS IT IS! A WHOLE WITH NO BORDERS OR BOUNDARIES!

THEN WE'D BRING THEM BACK AND.....
WHAT?
4-18

IT SEEMS ODD THAT AN EX-ASTRONAUT WOULD BECOME A POTATO FARMER IN THIS LITTLE TOWN....
OH, I DON'T KNOW....

SOMETHING HAPPENS OUT THERE IN SPACE. I'VE TALKED TO OTHER GUYS ABOUT IT. A LOT OF THEM REALLY CHANGED WHEN THEY GOT BACK....
REALLY?

YEAH! SOME WENT TO EXTREMES! THEY BECAME DRUNKS, ARTISTS, MYSTICS, TENT REVIVAL PREACHERS....
4-19

....CONGRESSMEN.....
WOW! THAT IS EXTREME!
I KNOW.

SO WHY'D YOU COME BACK TO THIS TOWN AFTER BEING IN OUTER SPACE?
WELL, I LEARNED IT DOESN'T SO MUCH MATTER WHERE YOU ARE.
SINCLAIR
4-20

I MEAN, I GOT BACK FROM THE MOON AND I STILL FELT LIKE THE UNIVERSE WAS RIGHT OVER MY HEAD. I MEAN, THE SKY'S RIGHT UP THERE....AND IT GOES ON FOREVER.

THE STARS, THE PLANETS,.... THEY'RE NOT IN BOOKS, OR ON TV, OR IN A TELESCOPE, THEY'RE RIGHT HERE IN THE SAME SPACE WE'RE IN, RIGHT NOW. SO...ONCE YOU'VE BEEN IN SPACE, IT'S LIKE YOU NEVER REALLY COME BACK BECAUSE THERE'S NO WHERE ELSE YOU CAN BE.

DOES NASA KNOW THIS?
I BRIEFED THEM....

LESSON ONE IN POWER WALKING.... SHOULDERS DOWN, TUCK THE CHIN, TIGHTEN THE STOMACH!

WHAT'S LESSON TWO?
SINCLAIR

WHOOPS!
ZIP!

IN LESSON TWO, YOU'LL LEARN TO CHEW GUM AT THE SAME TIME.....
4-22

I THINK YOU BETTER TELL CARL TO BACK OFF ON THE ORGANIC SAUERKRAUT.
WHY?
SINCLAIR

I THINK IT MIGHT CONSTITUTE AN ENVIRONMENTAL HAZARD!

WHY?
4-23

I THINK HE'S CONTRIBUTING TO THE GREENHOUSE EFFECT.
URP...
URP...URF...
OOFFF..
BURRFFF
BOOF!
ORF!
OOF
URP

YOU KNOW, IT SAYS HERE THERE'S A "12 STEP" SUPPORT GROUP NOW FOR PEOPLE WHO TALK TOO MUCH!
4-24
SINCLAIR

IT'S CALLED "ANDONANDON ANDON ANON".

HEY, GET ME A FLYSWATTER...... THERE'S A BUG IN HERE.

YOU'RE NOT GOING TO HURT IT, ARE YOU?

OF COURSE I'M GOING TO HURT IT!

BUT, MANY INSECTS ARE OUR FRIENDS!

HEY,...

YOUR SOCIAL LIFE IS YOUR BUSINESS!
WAP!
4-25
SINCLAIR

I TOLD YOU I DIDN'T LIKE THIS FANCY BOTTLED WATER! IT TASTES FUNNY!
OF COURSE!

THAT'S THE OFFICIAL BOTTLED WATER OF DESERT STORM!

"SCHWARZKOPF SPRINGS"?

RIGHT! YOU CAN TASTE THE DESERT DUST, THE SWEAT, THE CAMEL HAIR, THE ACRID SMELL OF ARTILLERY SMOKE.
WOW!
4-26
SINCLAIR

AND I THOUGHT THIS STUFF WAS FOR WIMPS!
OH, NO!, NOW IT'S PART OF OUR MILITARY ASSETS!

IT SAYS HERE THAT NEGATIVE THINKING CAN BE AN ADDICTION!
REALLY?!

YEAH! PEOPLE GET USED TO THAT "FIGHT OR FLIGHT" BLAST OF ADRENALIN WHEN THEY BEAT UP ON THEMSELVES!
NO!
SINCLAIR
4-27

HOW COME EVERYTHING I LIKE TO DO IS SOME KINDA DISEASE OR SOMETHING?

YOU LIKE BEING MISERABLE?
HEY! IT'S ONE OF MY ONLY REMAINING PLEASURES IN LIFE!

HEY! I GOT A LETTER FROM YURI, MY RUSSIAN PEN PAL!
WHAT'S HE SAY?

HE'S JOINING THE MOVEMENT TO A FREE ECONOMY!

HE'S GOT AN ENTRY LEVEL POSITION WITH A BIG AMERICAN COMPANY!
WHICH ONE?
SINCLAIR

... IN MOSCOW...
SO COMRADE, THAT'S TWO BURGERS, TWO FRIES, AND A LARGE COKE!.....
DA...
4·29

SO YOUR PEN PAL IS WORKING AT McDONALD'S IN MOSCOW?
YUP.

SO, HOW'S HE LIKE IT?
O.K., I GUESS. HE SAYS THAT SOME OF THE TRAINEES,...
SINCLAIR

STILL HAVE SOME BAD HABITS THEY NEED TO WORK ON....

TWO BEEG MACS PLEASE.....
OF COURSE, COMRADE,... MAY I SEE YOUR PAPERS, PLEASE.....
4·30

SO THEY REALLY LIKE THAT FAST FOOD OVER IN MOSCOW?
YEAH, ACCORDING TO YURI, IT'S A MOB SCENE EVERY DAY!

SO, COMRADE, YOU TAKE THE TRAIN INTO MOSCOW, YOU STAND IN LINE FOR 6 HOURS,.....
5·1

...WHAT DO LIKE SO MUCH ABOUT MOSCOW McDONALD'S?
I JUST CAN'T GET OVER THE FAST SERVICE!
SINCLAIR

WELCOME, COMRADE, TO McDONALD'S, THE CUTTING EDGE OF GLASNOST AND PERESTROIKA!
?
5-2

DO YOU WANT HAMBURGERS, FRENCH FRIES, MILKSHAKES, SALAD, McNUGGETS, McMUFFINS, COKE,.....

HAMBURGERS? I SAW THE BIG LINE AND JUST JUMPED INTO IT.....

...... I JUST ASSUMED IT WAS FOR CIGARETTES!
CIGARETTES?
ARE YOU SURE YOU DON'T HAVE ANY MARLBOROS?
SINCLAIR

... SO, I STILL HAVE MUCH TO LEARN ABOUT CAPITALISM...
5-3

AND SO DO MY COUNTRYMEN. AS YOU KNOW, THE ECONOMY HERE IS SO BAD....

....MANY PEOPLE ARE RELYING ENTIRELY ON BLACK MARKET BARTERING....

THAT'LL BE TWO AND A HALF RUBLES,.....
I'LL GIVE YOU TWO PACKS OF CAMELS AND A BAR OF SOAP.....

I'VE GOT TO WRITE TO YURI AND WARN HIM ABOUT HIS NEW BUSINESS! PEOPLE IN RUSSIA DON'T KNOW ABOUT THE HEALTH EFFECTS OF FAST FOOD YET......

SOMETHING HAS TO BE DONE TO STOP THE EXPORT OF AMERICA'S MOST DAMAGING PRODUCTS AND LIFESTYLES!

PERHAPS WE NEED A WHOLE NEW FORM OF DIPLOMACY!... I KNOW.....

.... WE'LL CALL IT,..... CHOLESTEROIKA!
5-4

SO WHERE ARE YOU GOING ON YOUR WEEK OFF?
HOME TO SEE THE FOLKS.

REALLY?
YUP, I HAVEN'T BEEN HOME SINCE I DROPPED OUT OF SCHOOL!
SINCLAIR 5-6

YOU TOLD ME ONCE THAT YOUR FATHER WAS REALLY CONSERVATIVE...
YUP. WE DON'T GET ALONG...

AS FAR AS HIS POLITICS, PUT IT THIS WAY..... MY DAD THINKS JESSE HELMS SHOULD BE BURIED IN THE KREMLIN WALL......
OH...

PERHAPS NOW THAT I'M MORE MATURE, MY PARENTS AND I CAN GET ALONG....

IN THE PAST, SO MANY TRIVIAL THINGS HAVE DIVIDED US. MAYBE AFTER THIS LONG SEPARATION.....

SINCLAIR 5-7

...THEY'LL BE ABLE TO FOCUS ON THE ESSENTIALS....

HI, MOM, I'M....
TAKE OFF THOSE FILTHY CLOTHES!

THE OLD PLACE IS SPOTLESS JUST THE WAY IT'S ALWAYS BEEN....

MOM WAS ALWAYS A NUT FOR NEATNESS...
5-8 SINCLAIR

SHE COULD PROBABLY GET A JOB FOR NASA CLEANING THE DUST FREE HANGARS... NO PARTICLE GREATER THAN ONE MICRON....

THE MASK AND GOWNS ARE SOMETHING NEW, EH MOM?
YOU'LL NEED A HAIRNET....

WELL, SON, I HAVE TO SAY, YOUR MOTHER AND I ARE MIGHTY DISAPPOINTED IN YOU.

YOU'VE BASICALLY DONE NOTHING CONSTRUCTIVE WITH YOUR LIFE SO FAR,...

GEE, POP, OTHER PEOPLE TELL ME I'M A PRETTY NICE GUY,...
"OTHER PEOPLE"!
5-9
ARE YOU GOING TO BE RULED BY WHAT "OTHER PEOPLE" SAY?
GEE, I GUESS NOT. SORRY...

SO TELL ME ABOUT THIS RESTAURANT YOU'VE BEEN WORKING IN.
IT'S SORT OF A HEALTH FOOD CAFE.
URF GULP

THAT'S NICE. I'VE BEEN TRYING TO GET YOUR FATHER TO EAT BETTER SINCE HIS HEART ATTACK. I GOT THIS DINNER PLAN TONITE OUT OF A "HEART SMART RECIPE BOOK"
MUNCH

PORK CHOPS WITH FRIED POTATOES AND GRAVY,... ROLLS AND BUTTER,... CHOCOLATE CAKE AND ICE CREAM,... THIS IS A "HEART SMART RECIPE"?
SLURP
5-10

BUT,...THERE'S NO CREAM CHEESE ON THE LIME JELLO!
OH, RIGHT,...
MUNCH...

HONESTLY, I DO THE BEST I CAN, BUT I JUST DON'T KNOW HOW TO GET YOUR FATHER TO EAT THE WAY HE SHOULD!

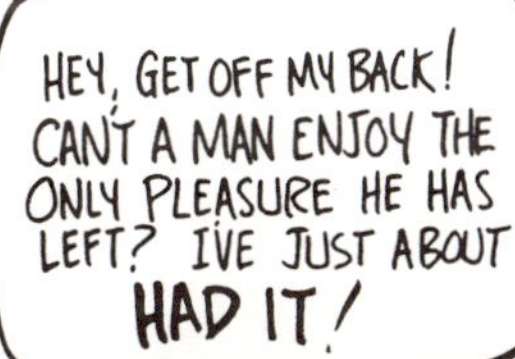

HEY, GET OFF MY BACK! CAN'T A MAN ENJOY THE ONLY PLEASURE HE HAS LEFT? I'VE JUST ABOUT HAD IT!

O.K., DON'T LISTEN TO ME, JUST GO RIGHT AHEAD! WHAT DO I CARE? GIVE YOURSELF ANOTHER HEART ATTACK! WHY SHOULD I DO THE EXTRA WORK!
THAT'S MORE LIKE IT!!

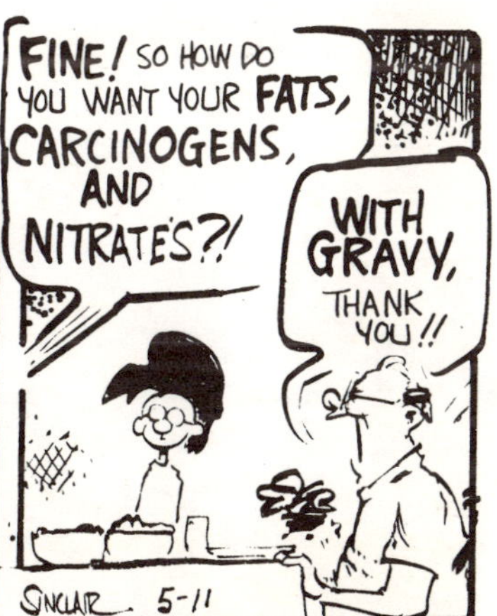

FINE! SO HOW DO YOU WANT YOUR FATS, CARCINOGENS, AND NITRATES?!
WITH GRAVY, THANK YOU!!
SINCLAIR 5-11

HOW 'BOUT TRYING OUR NEW 3.95$ SPECIAL NO FAT, NO CHOLESTEROL, NO PRESERVATIVES, BANANA SPLIT?
HEY,... THAT SOUNDS GOOD!

HERE YOU GO!

IT'S A BANANA.

IT'S A LOUSY BANANA! NO ICE CREAM! NO CHOCOLATE SAUCE! NO STRAWBERRY SYRUP! NO WHIPPED CREAM! NO MARASCHINO CHERRY!

WELL,... WE TOOK OUT ALL THAT YUCKY STUFF!

HOW CAN YOU CALL THIS A BANANA SPLIT?!!
I SPLIT IT MYSELF!

HEY CARL, MEET LITTLE EAGLE, HE WORKS AT THE HEALTH CLUB.
HI.
HI.

ARE YOU A REAL INDIAN?
WELL, ACTUALLY, I PREFER TO SAY I'M A NATIVE AMERICAN!

AFTER ALL, OUR PEOPLE HAVE BEEN HERE FOR AT LEAST 10,000 YEARS. ACTUALLY IT'S THE WHITE MAN WHO HASN'T REALLY BECOME AN AMERICAN YET!
REALLY?
5-13
SINCLAIR

YUP! YOU'RE STILL MOSTLY A BUNCH OF EUROPEANS WHO'RE LOST!

SO, LITTLE EAGLE, DO YOU THINK WE SHOULD BE SITTING HERE?
WHAT DO YOU MEAN?

WELL, THIS IS THE "NO SMOKE SIGNALS" SECTION!
NUDGE

HEH HEH HEH HA HA HO
5-14
SINCLAIR

DON'T MIND CARL. HE'S ALWAYS BEEN SOMEWHAT POLITICALLY INCORRECT.
IT'S O.K.
HEH HEH

YOU SEE, MY PEOPLE BELIEVE THAT ALL THE UNIVERSE IS A CIRCLE!

THE EARTH IS A CIRCLE! THE SKY IS A CIRCLE! THE LIFE OF A MAN IS A CIRCLE!
5-15
SINCLAIR

SOUNDS LIKE MUMBO JUMBO TO ME.

THE PROBLEM IS, CARL'S KIND OF A SQUARE.
I SEE.

CHECK OUT OUR NEWEST FEATURE ON THE MENU! FOR ALL OUR DAILY SPECIALS WE'VE GOT A SPECIAL SCRATCH AND SNIFF PAD.
MENU

TRY THE ONE ON TODAY'S LUNCHEON MENU, THE SAUERKRAUT EGGROLLS......

SCRATCH
MENU

SSSNIFFFF
MENU

IT REMINDS ME,..... I FORGOT TO TAKE A SHOWER THIS MORNING.
BUT DID YOU LIKE IT?
SINCLAIR
5-16

IT'S REALLY FRIGHTENING HOW MANY ANIMAL SPECIES ARE BECOMING EXTINCT!

AW, I'M NOT SO WORRIED.

AFTER ALL, WHAT DO WE NEED ANIMALS FOR, EXCEPT THE ONES WE EAT!

WELL, THE WAY THINGS ARE GOING, YOU'D BETTER LEARN TO LIKE THE TASTE OF COCKROACHES!
5-17

WHOAH! THAT'S DISGUSTING!

HOLY COW! I CAN'T BELIEVE HE'D SAY THAT ON TV!

WHAT ARE YOU WATCHING?
5-18
SINCLAIR

I DON'T KNOW. IT'S EITHER "WORLD NEWS TONIGHT", OR "AMERICA'S FUNNIEST PEOPLE."

IT GETS WORSE EVERY DAY!

NOWADAYS,.... EVERYBODY'S SOME KIND OF AMATEUR PSYCHOLOGIST!
5-20
SINCLAIR

HMMM.....

AND HOW DOES THAT MAKE YOU FEEL?
NOW DON'T START WITH ME...!!

RRRINGG
HELLO?

BREAKER... BREAKER... THIS IS BOY HOWDY CALLIN', C'MON....
YES?

BREAKER, BREAKER..... WHAT'S YER HANDLE GOOD BUDDY, C'MON,...
5-21
SINCLAIR

DID YOU PICK UP THE CELLULAR PHONE, DEAR?
THAT'S A BIG 10-4, GOOD BUDDY!

FEEL THE PAIN! MAKE IT BURN!

AGONY!! TORMENT!! TORTURE!!

YA GOTTA LOVE IT!
5-22
SINCLAIR

FITNESS GYM
SO WHAT'S NOT TO LOVE?

I'VE BEEN READING THIS BOOK ABOUT HERBAL REMEDIES.
HERB

IT SAYS, "FOR EVERY HUMAN MALADY, THERE IS A PLANT."
?
HERBS

HERBS
4-9

DOES IT LIST "DORKWEED" ANYWHERE?

SO, ALEX, DO YOU THINK LIFE BEGINS AT 40?

I DON'T KNOW YET.
5-24

LET'S ASK THE MAN WHO KNOWS... HEY, CARL,.... DOES LIFE BEGIN AT 40?

IT DOESN'T SO MUCH BEGIN,.. AS JUST KINDA DAWNS ON YA......

I THOUGHT I WOULD PLAY A LITTLE MUSIC FOR YOU. THIS HARP IS TUNED TO AN ANCIENT 5-NOTE SCALE.....

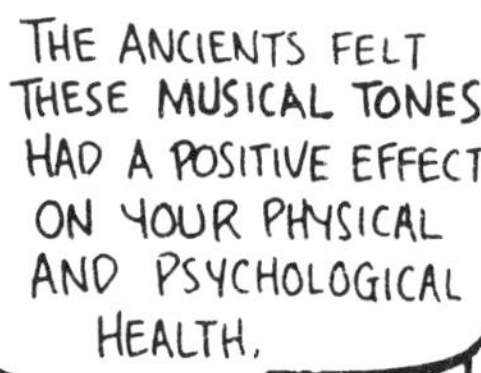
THE ANCIENTS FELT THESE MUSICAL TONES HAD A POSITIVE EFFECT ON YOUR PHYSICAL AND PSYCHOLOGICAL HEALTH.

SO, DO YOU KNOW "STAIRWAY TO HEAVEN"?
I SAID "ANCIENTS," NOT "OLDIES."
4-12

...AND A SAFE HAVEN FOR BIRDS AND WILDLIFE! IMAGINE, RIGHT HERE IN THE CITY, WILD ANIMALS LIKE THOSE FRIENDLY CHIPMUNKS THERE....

I'VE BEEN READING THIS BOOK ABOUT **HERBAL REMEDIES.**
HERB

IT SAYS, "FOR EVERY HUMAN MALADY, THERE IS A **PLANT.**"
?
HERBS

HERBS
4-9

DOES IT LIST "**DORKWEED**" ANYWHERE?

ECOLOGY TEACHES US MANY PROFOUND TRUTHS!

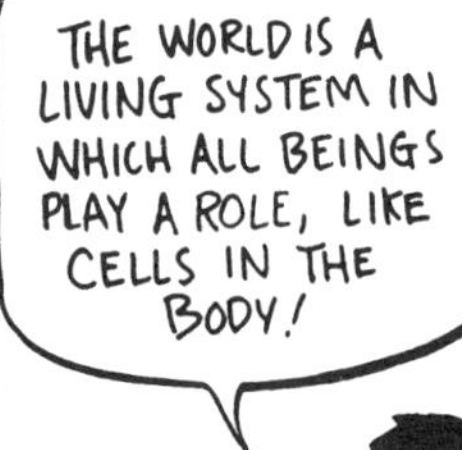
THE WORLD IS A LIVING SYSTEM IN WHICH ALL BEINGS PLAY A ROLE, LIKE CELLS IN THE BODY!

5-31

EACH OF US IS A SMALL BUT VITAL PART OF A **HUGE SEAMLESS WHOLE!**
SLURP

FINE, FINE,... JUST LEAVE ME **OUT** OF IT.
I'M NOT SURE THAT'S AN OPTION.

YOU KNOW, THE AVERAGE MAN PROBABLY USES ONLY **10%** OF HIS **BRAIN CAPACITY!...**

IMAGINE. IT'S LIKE OWNING A MAGNIFICENT ITALIAN RACING CAR AND NEVER TAKING IT OUT OF THE DRIVEWAY!

RIGHT. BUT THEN...
6-1

...I DON'T IMAGINE YOU'VE GOTTEN TOO MANY **SPEEDING TICKETS** YOURSELF.

YOU KNOW, I'VE LEARNED SOME LESSONS IN MY TIME, ... AND I ALWAYS TELL PEOPLE.....

THE THREE MOST IMPORTANT THINGS IN LIFE......
6-3
SINCLAIR

... WORK HARD,.... AND BE TOUGH!

CERTAINLY A PROFOUND MESSAGE FOR US ALL TO CONSIDER.....

QUICK! I'M IN A RUSH, BUT I NEED A QUICK MEAL!

DON'T WORRY! I'VE GOT A "BUSINESSMAN'S QUICK SPECIAL! IT'S A TOSSED SALAD, SOUP, VEGGIE STIR FRY,

CABBAGE ROLL, PASTA SIDE DISH, AND A MUFFIN.......
... I DON'T HAVE TIME TO EAT ALL THAT!!!

OH, DON'T WORRY, WE PUT IT IN A BLENDER SO YOU DONT HAVE TO CHEW IT!
GREAT!
6-4

T.V. GETS WORSE EVERY SEASON!
T.V.

AW, YOU'RE JUST A SNOB!

YOU THINK T.V. SHOULD HAVE SOME KINDA' HIGH INTELLECTUAL CONTENT!
?
SINCLAIR 6-5

YEAH, WHAT'S WRONG WITH THE LOWEST COMMON DEHUMANIZER?
YEAH! WHAT'S THE BIG DEAL?

YOU KNOW WHAT'S WRONG WITH PEOPLE IN THIS COUNTRY? THEY'RE NOT IN TOUCH WITH THEIR BODIES!

LIKE, THEY DON'T KNOW HOW TO READ THEIR OWN INTERNAL SIGNALS FOR WHEN TO EAT!

OH C'MON THAT'S EASY!!
6-6
SINCLAIR

DURING THE COMMERCIALS!

PROBLEMS, PROBLEMS, ... NOTHING BUT PROBLEMS EVERY DAY!

BUT..... PROBLEMS AREN'T NECESSARILY BAD!
6-7
SINCLAIR

TRY TO LOOK AT EACH PROBLEM AS AN OPPORTUNITY TO GROW!

WELL,..MY MAIN PROBLEM IS THAT YOU'RE AN INCOMPETENT BOOB!
HEY, NO PROBLEM!

HERE, TRY THIS.

THE MAXIMUM POSSIBLE FIBER, BRAN, AND ROUGHAGE SALAD.

IT'S NATURE'S PERFECT CLEANSER!
6-8
SINCLAIR

WHY NOT JUST SWALLOW A BRILLO PAD?

GREETINGS, ALEX! HAVE I GOT NEWS FOR YOU! HOW WOULD YOU LIKE TO TURN YOUR LIFE AROUND?
HUH?

I'M NOW A CERTIFIED INSTRUCTOR OF AMERICA'S MOST POPULAR MOTIVATIONAL TRAINING COURSE.... THE DALE BARNUMBEE SEMINAR!
OH?
SINCLAIR

YUP. IT'S CHANGED MY LIFE. IT'S A WHOLE NEW WAY TO SEE THE WORLD AND LIFE, AND MONEY, AND SALES, AND PROSPERITY CONSCIOUSNESS!...
...OR "PROS CON" AS WE CALL IT.
OH, YEAH.
6-17

THE REASON I'M TEACHING THE "DALE BARNUMBEE COURSE" IS THAT SO MANY PEOPLE TODAY DON'T UNDERSTAND THE "LAWS OF WEALTH AND PROSPERITY".
SINCLAIR

EVERYWHERE YOU GO TODAY PEOPLE TALK ABOUT DOOM AND GLOOM! I USED TO BE THE SAME WAY, BUT THEN...

...THE DALE BARNUMBEE COURSE TAUGHT ME THAT OPPORTUNITIES ARE ALWAYS OUT THERE IF YOU'RE WILLING TO TAKE ADVANTAGE OF THEM!
6-18

RIGHT. LIKE, THERE'S AN OPPORTUNITY BORN EVERY MINUTE.
NOW, THAT'S WHAT I CALL PROSPERITY THINKING!

YOU SEE, THE "DALE BARNUMBEE PROSPERITY TRAINING COURSE" ALL COMES FROM ONE FUNDAMENTAL INSIGHT! DALE BARNUMBEE KNEW THAT EINSTEIN PROVED MATTER IS ENERGY!

...WELL, IT FOLLOWS THAT ENERGY IS MOVEMENT.... MOVEMENT IS CHANGE... CHANGE IS TIME..........
© 1991 by King Features Syndicate, Inc. World rights reserved

NOW, TIME, OF COURSE, IS MONEY.... AND FINALLY,
WAIT, DON'T TELL ME........MONEY..... MONEY TALKS!!
EXACTLY!
WOW! COSMIC! I GUESS THE MOST PROFOUND TRUTHS ARE THE SIMPLEST!
SINCLAIR
6-19

SO THE IMPORTANT THING TO REMEMBER IS THAT YOUR MIND CREATES YOUR REALITY!

IF YOU BELIEVE IT, YOU CAN ACHIEVE IT! IF YOU CAN DREAM IT YOU CAN DO IT!
SINCLAIR
IF YOU DESIRE IT, YOU CAN ACQUIRE IT!
COOL! HOW 'BOUT, IF YOU WING IT, YOU CAN SWING IT!
6-20

IF YOU SHAKE IT,... YOU CAN BAKE IT!...
WELL, HEY,... IF YOU WANT IT YOU CAN HAVE IT.

THANKS FOR HELPING US TEST OUR NEW WORKOUT MACHINE!
SINCLAIR

IT'S A MEGA-FLEX MODEL X-5000 "ULTRA PUMP."
6-21

BUT WE JUST CALL IT,... "THE WIDOWMAKER."...

I GUESS I NEED TO PAY MORE ATTENTION TO THE NEWS.
6-22

THE WORLD'S ENVIRONMENTAL PROBLEMS ARE REACHING A CRITICAL LEVEL. I NEED TO INFORM MYSELF MORE.

I NEED TO STEP UP AND PLAY MY PART!

AFTER ALL, I BELONG ON THIS PLANET, ITS MY HOME!
THAT YOU'LL HAVE TO PROVE.

VIDEO SMASH
DO YOU HAVE YOUR MEMBERSHIP CARD?
OH, YEAH!

LET'S SEE,..VIDEO DOME, VIDEO ALLEY, CASTLE VIDEO, VIDEO PALACE, VIDEO BARN, VIDEO GALLERY, VIDEO BUSTER, MAGIC VIDEO, KING'S VIDEO, VIDEO DEN, VIDEO RANCH, VIDEO SQUARE,...
SINCLAIR 6-24

VIDEO SHACK, VIDEO ZOOM, VIDEO ROOM, VIDEO STACK, VIDEO RACK, SUPER VIDEO, MANIC VIDEO, VIDEO SLAM,....

VIDEO VIEW, VIDEO LIGHT, VIDEO SWAMP, IDIO-VIDIO, MONTEVIDEO VIDEO, VIDEO RODEO,.....
NEVER MIND, JUST TAKE IT....

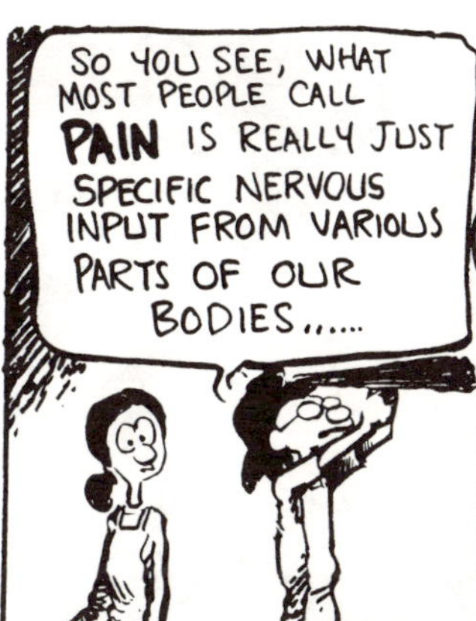
SO YOU SEE, WHAT MOST PEOPLE CALL PAIN IS REALLY JUST SPECIFIC NERVOUS INPUT FROM VARIOUS PARTS OF OUR BODIES......

I PREFER TO THINK OF PAIN AS VERY HIGH QUALITY INFORMATION!
BEANS

WHONK
6-25
SINCLAIR

HOW DO YOU FEEL?
VERY WELL INFORMED,.. THANK YOU.

SEE, MY PHILOSOPHY IS THAT FOOD SHOULD BE GUILT FREE. WHEN PEOPLE ARE HUNGRY, THEY SHOULD EAT!

WHAT? ARE YOU CRAZY? PEOPLE DON'T EAT MY COOKIES WHEN THEY'RE HUNGRY! THEY EAT WHEN THEY'RE ANGRY, BORED, TIRED, OR LONELY!

EAT WHEN YOU'RE HUNGRY? ARE YOU NUTS? THE ECONOMY WOULD GRIND TO A HALT!

LIKE,.... WOW HAVE YOU GOT A LOT TO LEARN,..... HUNGRY? WHOAH, BABY!!
IT WAS JUST A THOUGHT.
6-26
SINCLAIR

OOPS! SORRY, CARL.

BEFORE YOU SAY ANYTHING, I THINK YOU SHOULD ASK YOURSELF, WHAT CAN I LEARN FROM THIS,....

WHAT IS THIS EXPERIENCE TELLING ME?...
SINCLAIR 6-27

WELL, FOR ONE THING,... THAT YOU'RE STILL USING TOO MUCH GARLIC!

WAR, DISEASE, FAMINE, DISASTER,....

IT'S SO COMMON IN THE NEWS WE DON'T EVEN NOTICE IT!
SO?

WELL, WHAT IF WE'RE ALL BECOMING SO DESENSITIZED IT DOESN'T AFFECT US.
6-28
SINCLAIR

DON'T LET IT BOTHER YA. YA DON'T SEE ME CRYIN' ABOUT IT, DO YA?
OH, YEAH. MAYBE YOU'RE RIGHT.

WOW!

LITTLE EAGLE'S BEEN TELLING ME THE STORY OF HOW HIS TRIBE GOT STARTED WITH THE HELP OF THE BEARS, BUFFALO, AND EAGLES!

OH, YEAH,.... THOSE ARE ALL JUST OLD MYTHS.

THAT'S THE TROUBLE WITH YOU EUROPEANS...

...YOU THINK JUST BECAUSE SOMETHING NEVER HAPPENED,... THAT IT'S NOT TRUE!
6-29

I CAN'T **STAND IT!** THE DARN **GOVERNMENT** IS TAKING THIS COUNTRY RIGHT DOWN THE **TUBE!**

YOU KNOW WHAT I'D DO IF I WAS **PRESIDENT? FIRE EVERYBODY! THAT'S** WHAT!

THEN WHAT?
THEN,... I'D QUIT!
7-1
SINCLAIR

OOPS!
CRASH!
TINKLE

AGAIN? DON'T YOU EVER **LEARN** FROM YOUR MISTAKES?
SINCLAIR 7-2

BUT,.... PICASSO SAID WE SHOULDN'T WORRY ABOUT OUR MISTAKES! THEY **MAKE** US WHAT WE **ARE!**

YOU MUST BE **MISTAKEN!**
THANKS. I TRY.

GLAD YOU DECIDED TO TRY THE **TANNING BOOTH!**
SOLAR-TRON

MIND IF I PUT THESE IN WITH YOU?

POTATOES?
RIGHT. MY LUNCH.
7-3
SINCLAIR

WHEN **THEY'RE** DONE,.... **YOU'RE** DONE... ENJOY!
BUT....
SLAM
CLIK!

HEY, WAITER! WHAT'S THIS STUFF?

AND THIS? AND WHAT ABOUT **THIS?**
7-4
SINCLAIR

HERE. READ THIS.

MOST RESTAURANTS JUST HAVE MENUS. WE HAVE "**INTERPRETIVE FACT SHEETS.**"

C'MON IN! WELCOME! YOU'RE JUST IN TIME!

WELCOME TO ANOTHER AFTERNOON "STRESS BUSTER."

BY NOW YOU SHOULD ALL BE GETTING YOUR **COOKIES AND MILK.**

WHEN YOU'RE DONE, GO AHEAD AND PUT YOUR **HEAD DOWN!**
7-5

OTHER PLACES HAVE FRIDAY AFTERNOON "HAPPY HOUR".... WE HAVE "**NAPPY HOUR**".

HERE YOU GO, FRESH ALFALFA SPROUTS!

ONE OF NATURE'S OWN **LIVING FOODS!**

WAP WAP WAP WAP

I JUST DON'T WANT TO EAT ANYTHING THAT'S NOT **DEAD** YET.
SINCLAIR

© 1991 by
TRENDS OF THE 90'S
AS "RAINFOREST CHIC" BECOMES MORE WIDESPREAD,... LOOK FOR "DOLPHIN SWIMS" TO GIVE WAY TO...."THE PYTHON EXPERIENCE"....
WOW! I FEEL A MUCH DEEPER CONNECTION TO THE FOOD CHAIN!
7-15
SINCLAIR

UGH. DEPRESSED AGAIN.
SINCLAIR 7-16

THAT'S NOT ALL BAD. THE DARK SIDE OF YOUR SUBCONSCIOUS MAY BE SENDING YOU A MESSAGE!

DARK SIDE? SUBCONSCIOUS? I DON'T HAVE ANY OF THAT WEIRDO STUFF.

I'M JUST A COMPLETELY NORMAL, REGULAR GUY. ALWAYS HAVE BEEN!
WHOA! THAT'S A BAD SIGN!

HEY, CARL! GUESS WHAT? LITTLE EAGLE'S GOING TO TEACH ME SOME OF HIS TRADITIONAL SKILLS!
YES, WE'VE BEGUN WITH THE ANCIENT TRACKING SKILLS OF MY ANCESTORS. THEY COULD READ VOLUMES IN A CLOD OF DIRT, OR A LEAF....

FOR INSTANCE, TELL US WHAT YOU SEE IN THE SAND AND SCUFF MARKS ON THIS FLOOR....
HMMM...

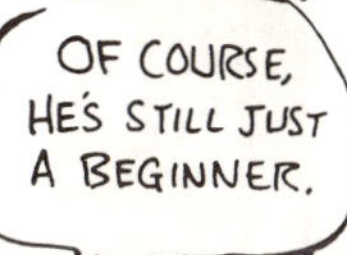

MANY HORSES, MEN WITH RIFLES, ... TWO, MAYBE THREE DAYS RIDE....
OF COURSE, HE'S STILL JUST A BEGINNER.
SINCLAIR 7-17

HEY! WHAT'S THE DEAL! THIS CEREAL IS BLUE!

OF COURSE! IT'S MADE FROM BLUE CORN!... THE ANCIENT, SACRED GRAIN OF THE HOPIS...
7-18
SINCLAIR

HEY, CRANBROOK YOU CAN PITCH ALL THESE CORNFLAKES. THEY'RE ALL BLUE AND MOLDY!

OF COURSE, A REAL HOPI WOULD PROBABLY HAVE PICKED UP ON THAT SOONER...

YOU KNOW WHAT YOUR PROBLEM IS? YOU'RE LAZY! THAT'S WHAT!
?

BUT I THINK LAZINESS ISN'T ALWAYS BAD. SOMETIMES A LITTLE LAZINESS IS JUST WHAT WE NEED TO KEEP US FROM DOING SOMETHING SILLY!

LIKE WHAT?
LIKE WORK!
7-19

WELL, AM I RIGHT?
I'M THINKING! I'M THINKING!

O.K., TELL ME AGAIN ONE LAST TIME, WHY YOU WEAR THAT GOOFY OUTFIT!
SIMPLE! I HELP PEOPLE LIGHTEN UP!
SINCLAIR
7-20

GOOD HUMOR IS JUST AS IMPORTANT FOR YOUR BODY AS GOOD FOOD!

YOU MEAN, I NOT ONLY GOT TO CHANGE EVERYTHING I EAT, I'VE GOTTA BE HAPPY ABOUT IT?
OH, YEAH! IT'S VITAL!

IN FACT, THEY SAY "BEER AND FRANKS WITH CHEER AND THANKS IS BETTER THAN SPROUTS AND BREAD WITH DOUBTS AND DREAD!
NOW YOU TELL ME!

POLLUTION! WAR! DRUGS! POISON GAS! NUCLEAR WEAPONS!

SOME DAY IT'S ALL GONNA REALLY HIT THE FAN, Y'KNOW!

YES, I THINK IT'S POSSIBLE THAT ONE DAY THE HUMAN RACE MAY DESTROY ITSELF.

....AND BE REPLACED BY A KINDER, GENTLER, SPECIES.

YOU MEAN,... LIKE REPUBLICANS?
YEAH,... OR MAYBE GILA MONSTERS.

About the Cartoonist

Peter Sinclair is a cartoonist/illustrator/paramedic/nurse/shiatsu therapist living in Midland, Michigan. He is by all accounts a righteous dude and a real stand-up guy. His two beautiful children want you to buy this book so that he can spend more time at home with them and their mother. Peter is also the editor of *King, Warrior, Magician, Weenie: Contemporary Men's Humor*.